# Communications in Computer and Information Science    **668**

*Commenced Publication in 2007*
Founding and Former Series Editors:
Alfredo Cuzzocrea, Dominik Ślęzak, and Xiaokang Yang

## Editorial Board

More information about this series at http://www.springer.com/series/7899

Muyun Yang · Shujie Liu (Eds.)

# Machine Translation

12th China Workshop, CWMT 2016
Urumqi, China, August 25–26, 2016
Revised Selected Papers

 Springer

*Editors*
Muyun Yang
Harbin Institute of Technology
Harbin
China

Shujie Liu
Microsoft Research Asia
Beijing
China

ISSN 1865-0929          ISSN 1865-0937  (electronic)
Communications in Computer and Information Science
ISBN 978-981-10-3634-7          ISBN 978-981-10-3635-4  (eBook)
DOI 10.1007/978-981-10-3635-4

Library of Congress Control Number: 2016963154

Printed on acid-free paper

This Springer imprint is published by Springer Nature
The registered company is Springer Nature Singapore Pte Ltd.
The registered company address is: 152 Beach Road, #21-01/04 Gateway East, Singapore 189721, Singapore

# Preface

Following the previous successful workshops in the series, the 12th China Workshop on Machine Translation (CWMT) was held during August 25–26, 2016, in Urumqi, China. This workshop provides an opportunity for researchers and practitioners to communicate and exchange ideas, and aims to improve the research of machine translation in China.

We were absolutely thrilled that 76 submissions were submitted to the conference. All of them were carefully reviewed in a double-blind manner and each paper was assigned to at least two independent reviewers. Finally, 15 Chinese and nine English papers were accepted, yielding an overall acceptation rate of 31.6%. With an English version of one Chinese paper, this proceedings volume comprises ten publications. As is traditionally the case with CWMT, the papers cover a wide range of subjects, including statistical MT, hybrid MT, MT evaluation, post editing, alignment, as well as inducing bilingual knowledge from corpora.

This year, CWMT 2016 featured three keynote speeches delivered by renowned experts in the field of MT and four invited talks exploring edge-cutting technologies by young researchers. A common topic that was highlighted in these talks is the emergence of neural-based MT paradigms, seemingly overtaking the statistical MT approach that first appeared in this conference 11 years ago.

There are a number of people we would like to thank. Firstly, this conference would not have been possible without the enormous efforts of Dr. Chengqing Zong, Dr. Le Sun, Prof. Tiejun Zhao, Prof. Jingbo Zhu, and Prof. Xiaodong Shi. We would especially like to thank the Springer for publishing the proceedings again (for the second time in CWMT series). Secondly, our heartfelt thanks go to Prof. Zhang Min, the general chair, and the members of the Program Committee, who, as usual, did sterling work over and above what might have reasonably been expected from them. Finally, we would like to thank Dr. Yating Yang and her team in Xinjiang Technical Institute of Physics and Chemistry, CAS, whose excellent conference organization impressed the attendees of CWMT 2016.

August 2016                                                                                       Muyun Yang

# Organization

## Steering Committee

Chengqing Zong    Institute of Automation of Chinese Academy of Sciences, China
Le Sun    Institute of Software Chinese Academy of Sciences, China
Tiejun Zhao    Harbin Institute of Technology, China
Jingbo Zhu    Northeastern University, China
Xiaodong Shi    Xiamen University, China

## Conference Chair

Min Zhang    Soochow University, China

## Program Chair

Muyun Yang    Harbin Institute of Technology, China

## Publication Chair

Shujie Liu    Microsoft Research Asia

## Program Committee

Hailong Cao    Harbin Institute of Technology, China
Yidong Chen    Xiamen University, China
Yufeng Chen    Beijing Jiaotong University, China
Chong Feng    Beijing Institute of Technology, China
Yuhang Guo    Beijing Institute of Technology, China
Yanqing He    Institute of Scientific and Technical Information of China, China
Zhongjun He    Baidu, Inc.
Shujian Huang    Nanjing University, China
Wenbin Jiang    Institute of Computing Technology,
       Chinese Academy of Sciences, China
Hongfei Jiang    Dinfo Beijing Technology Development Co., Ltd., China
Jianfeng Li    USTC iflytek Co., Ltd.
Lemao Liu    National Institute of Information and Communications
       Technology, China
Shujie Liu    Microsoft Research Asia
Yang Liu    Tsinghua University
Weihua Luo    Alibaba Inc.
Cunli Mao    Kunming University of Science and Technology

| | |
|---|---|
| Haitao Mi | IBM T.J. Watson Research Center, USA |
| Hideya Mino | National Institute of Information and Communications Technology |
| Jinsong Su | Xiamen University, China |
| Zhaopeng Tu | Noah's Ark Lab |
| Tong Xiao | Northeastern University |
| Deyi Xiong | Soochow University, China |
| Mo Yu | IBM T.J. Watson Research Center, USA |
| Yating Yang | Xinjiang Technical Institute of Physics and Chemistry Chinese Academy of Sciences, China |
| Conghui Zhu | Harbin Institute of Technology, China |
| Hao Zhang | Google, Inc. |
| Jiajun Zhang | Institute of Automation of Chinese Academy of Sciences, China |
| Yu Zhou | Institute of Automation of Chinese Academy of Sciences, China |
| Yun Zhu | Beijing Normal University, China |

## Local Organization Chair

| | |
|---|---|
| Yating Yang | Xinjiang Technical Institute of Physics and Chemistry, Chinese Academy of Sciences, China |

## Local Organizing Committee

| | |
|---|---|
| Xiaobo Wang | Xinjiang Technical Institute of Physics and Chemistry, Chinese Academy of Sciences, China |
| Wei Yang | Xinjiang Technical Institute of Physics and Chemistry, Chinese Academy of Sciences, China |
| Rui Dong | Xinjiang Technical Institute of Physics and Chemistry, Chinese Academy of Sciences, China |
| Chenggang Mi | Xinjiang Technical Institute of Physics and Chemistry, Chinese Academy of Sciences, China |
| Kamali | Xinjiang Technical Institute of Physics and Chemistry, Chinese Academy of Sciences, China |

## Organizers

Chinese Information Processing Society of China

## Co-organizer

Xinjiang Technical Institute of Physics and Chemistry, Chinese Academy of Sciences

## Sponsors

GTC Technology Co., Ltd.

Shenyang YaTrans Network Technology Co., Ltd.

Guangxi Daring E-Commerce Services Co., Ltd.

Beijing Lingosail Tech Co., Ltd.

# Contents

# MinKSR: A Novel MT Evaluation Metric for Coordinating Human Translators with the CAT-Oriented Input Method

Guoping Huang[1,2(✉)], Chunlu Zhao[3], Hongyuan Ma[3], Yu Zhou[1],
and Jiajun Zhang[1]

[1] National Laboratory of Pattern Recognition, Institute of Automation,
Chinese Academy of Sciences, Beijing, China
{guoping.huang,yzhou,jjzhang}@nlpr.ia.ac.cn
[2] University of Chinese Academy of Sciences, Beijing, China
[3] CNCERT/CC, Beijing, China
chunluzhao@cert.org.cn, mahongyuan@foxmail.com

**Abstract.** In order to improve the efficiency of human translation, there is an increasing interest in applying machine translation (MT) to computer assisted translation (CAT). The newly proposed CAT-oriented input method is such a typical approach, which can help translators significantly save keystrokes by exploiting MT deep information, such as n-best candidates, hypotheses and translation rules. In order to further save more keystrokes, we propose in this paper a novel MT evaluation metric for coordinating human translators with the input method. This evaluation metric takes MT deep information into account, and makes longer perfect fragments correspond to fewer keystrokes. Extensive experiments show that the novel evaluation metric makes MT substantially reduce the keystrokes of translating process by accurately grasping deep information for the CAT-oriented input method, and it significantly improves the productivity of human translation compared with BLEU and TER.

## 1 Introduction

Computer assisted translation (CAT) is a common way on language translation in which a human translator uses a software to perform and facilitate the translation process. In order to improve the efficiency of human translations, bridging machine translation (MT) and CAT has drawn more and more attention. For instance, the newly proposed CAT-oriented input method, which is called CoCat in [7], is such a typical approach. The input method can exploit deep information used by the underlying statistical machine translation (SMT) system, including translation rules, decoding hypotheses and n-best candidates, to significantly save keystrokes and speed up translating for languages with complex characters, such as Chinese and Japanese. In the CAT scenario, MT results vary considerably in quality. As a result, the most notable advantage of the CAT-oriented input method is that translators don't have to proofread such MT results.

© Springer Nature Singapore Pte Ltd. 2016
M. Yang and S. Liu (Eds.): CWMT 2016, CCIS 668, pp. 1–13, 2016.
DOI: 10.1007/978-981-10-3635-4_1

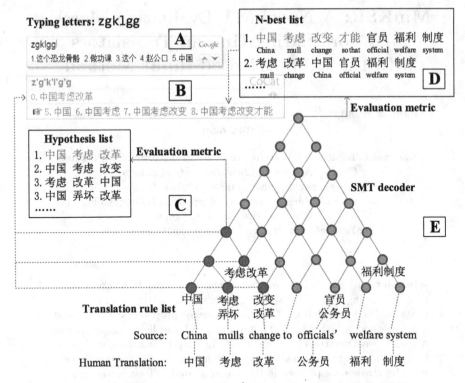

**Fig. 1.** The overview of CoCat input method and MT evaluation metric.

- Each node in the SMT decoder refers to a decoding span.
- The Chinese phrases below nodes refer to phrase translation rules and hypotheses during SMT decoding.

According to [7], Fig. 1 demonstrates how the CoCat input method works in translation from English to Chinese. In Zone A, if the translator adopts the wildly accepted Google Pinyin to perform translation from scratch, the abbreviated Chinese typing letters "zgklgg" (the acronym Chinese Pinyin) cannot elicit the correct translation. Because the Google Pinyin can not perceive what exactly the current user translating. Instead, in Zone B, the CoCat input method can correctly decode the same abbreviated letters into the desired result ("中国考虑改革", China considers to reform) with the help of translation rules and hypotheses (in Zone C), all of which are used by the underlying SMT decoder (in Zone E). What's more, the CoCat input method provides an n-gram prediction list (5-based ordinal in Zone B) based on the n-best list (in Zone D) provided by the SMT decoder. In this way, the CAT-oriented input method greatly improves the productivity of human translation.

And the input method has a lot of root for improvements in keystrokes saving. It needs to be further upgraded. As we can see, both the input method decoding results and the n-gram prediction lists heavily depend on the intermediate and final MT results, such as n-best candidates, hypotheses and translation rules. Obviously, better MT results can help the CAT-oriented input method.

In order to coordinate human translators with the CAT-oriented input method, it raises the question of how to generate and rank the intermediate and final MT results. Inspired by Fig. 1, the most natural way is to select a more appropriate MT evaluation metric. Under the guidance of a better evaluation metric, the SMT decoder is expected to generate more suitable deep information required by the CAT-oriented input method, and human translators can have higher efficiency.

However, almost all the evaluation metrics, such as BLEU [12], TER [13], KSR [11] and KSMR [1], do not take such useful deep information into account.

To achieve our goals, we propose in this paper a novel MT evaluation metric which considers deep information used by the underlying MT system, including n-best candidates, hypotheses and translation rules. It makes longer perfect fragments embedded in deep information correspond to fewer keystrokes. We call this metric MinKSR: Minimum Keystroke Saving Ratio. The word "minimum" means that the value of MinKSR shows how many keystrokes can be saved at least. The higher the value of MinKSR, the more the keystrokes can be saved.

With the guidance of MinKSR, the MT system is tuned to generate the most "suited" deep information from the point of view of the CAT-oriented input method, rather than the general "best" final results in terms of BLEU and TER. That is to say, MinKSR is a special MT evaluation metric for coordinating human translators with the CAT-oriented input methods.

In contrast, MinKSR aims at estimating the minimum keystrokes that can be saved by the underlying MT system to complete typing the translation using the CAT-oriented input method. So far as we know, MinKSR is the first MT evaluation metric for the CAT-based input method.

In summary, this paper makes the following contributions:

(1) MinKSR evaluates both the final MT results and the intermediate MT results, including n-best candidates, hypotheses and translation rules.
(2) Under the guidance of MinKSR, the MT system generates more useful deep information for coordinating human translators with the CAT-oriented input method. It helps the input method substantially and firmly reduce the keystrokes of translating process.
(3) MinKSR is an upgraded version of BLEU. It optimizes the intermediate MT results required by the CAT-oriented input method, while the BLEU scores of the final MT results don't really change.

## 2   Background

In Fig. 1, the SMT decoder scores translation rules, translation hypotheses and n-best candidates using a linear model. Generally speaking, the features of the

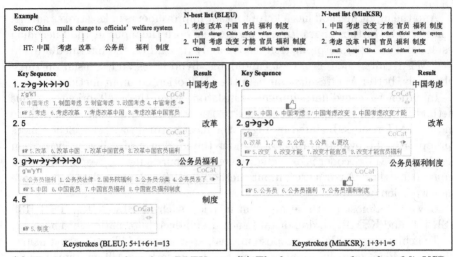

(a) The key sequence based on BLEU        (b) The key sequence based on MinKSR

**Fig. 2.** The comparison of key sequences based on the MT tuned by BLEU and MinKSR.

linear model are the probabilities from language models, translation models, and reordering models, plus other features. Tuning is the process of finding the optimal weights for this linear model. In the SMT tuning process, the performance of MT system is usually measured with a certain evaluation metric which compares the final MT results with the specified references. And then, during SMT decoding, the optimal weights directly influence the deep information required by the CAT-oriented input method.

The existing MT evaluation metrics, including BLEU, TER, KSR and KSMR, failed to cover such deep information. The well-known corpus-level metric BLEU is based on the n-gram matching between the final MT output and the reference translations. Another popular metric TER measures the amount of editing needed in modifying the MT output to exactly match a reference translation, and works well in the post-editing scenario [2,10,16]. KSR (keystroke ratio) and KSMR (keystroke ratio plus mouse-action ratio) is used to estimate the effort needed, especially in the IMT scenario [4], to produce correct translations. Besides, KSMR and KSR don't take account of languages with complex characters, for which an input method is required, such as Chinese and Japanese.

In the CAT scenario with the input method, we find that translators prefer to directly select the correct n-gram predictions. As a result, it is important to generate the perfect beginnings and longer matched fragments, even if the scores of BLEU or TER don't really change.

To illustrate how MinKSR works in the CAT scenario, let's consider the example in Fig. 2. The human translation refers to the target sentence in mind. For the sake of simplicity, deep information of the SMT decoder and the full n-best candidates are omitted. As we can see, it takes 13 keystrokes to input the human translation with the MT system tuned by BLEU as shown in Fig. 2(a).

In contrast, in Fig. 2(b), the number of keystrokes will be reduced to 5 by using MinKSR. The key is Step 1 and 3. Step 1 generates the ideal prediction "中国考虑" by grasping the perfect beginning fragment. And Step 3 hits the perfect prediction ("公务员福利制度", the welfare system of civil service) by searching the optimized MT deep information. This indicates that the deep information is very important for coordinating human translators with the CAT-oriented input method.

## 3   The MinKSR Metric

The purpose of MinKSR metric is to measure how many keystrokes can be reduced at least by the MT system integrated in the MT-based input method. The core idea of MinKSR is to map the longer perfect fragments to fewer keystrokes. To automatically evaluate the MT system, MinKSR is calculated by the empirical keystrokes rather than the practical keystrokes. There are three sufficient statistics to calculate MinKSR:

(1) $mk_{norm}(t_1^m)$: the count of minimum keystrokes to input the human translation $t_1^m = t_1 t_2 \dots t_m$ using the general input method character-by-character without the aid of the MT system.
(2) $ek(Q, t_1^m)$: the count of empirical keystrokes to input the human translation $t_1^m$ using the MT-based input method with the aid of the intermediate and final MT result $Q$.
(3) $pk(t_1^m)$: the count of minimum ideal keystrokes to input the human translation $t_1^m$ using the MT input method with the aid of the perfect MT candidate $c_1^n = t_1^m$.

Let $s_1^j = s_1 s_2 \dots s_j$ denotes the source sentence, $C$ denotes the n-best list $\{c_1^n = c_1 c_2 \dots c_n\}_1^{Z_1}$, $H$ denotes the hypothesis lists $\{h_1^{Z_2}\}$, and $L$ denotes the translation rule lists $\{l_1^{Z_3}\}$, where $j$ refers to the word number of source sentence, $Z_1$ refers to the length limitation of the n-best list, $Z_2$ refers to the length limitation of the hypothesis list for each phrase, $Z_3$ refers to the length limitation of the translation rule list for each phrase. Then the MT intermediate and final result can be defined as the triple $Q = (C, H, L)$. And the number of phrases is $\frac{j \times (j+1)}{2}$ for phrase-based SMT systems. Given the reference translation $t_1^m = t_1 t_2 \dots t_m$ of the source sentence, MinKSR, $r$, is given as follows:

$$r(Q, t_1^m) = \frac{mk_{norm}(t_1^m) - ek(Q, t_1^m)}{mk_{norm}(t_1^m) - pk(t_1^m)} \tag{1}$$

If there is only the candidate $c_1^n = c_1 c_2 \dots c_n$ in the MT result without depth information, MinKSR degenerates into a general MT evaluation metric and performs similarly to BLEU. If there is more than one reference, we just simply select the minimum $ek(Q, t_1^m)$. To calculate the three terms in Eq. 1, we introduce the following notations:

- $sn$: the character number of separators between words. $sn = 0$ for Chinese, $sn = 1$ for English (the space between words).
- $kc$: the count of keystrokes to select a certain candidate or prediction from the input method. In general, $kc = 1$ without page turning.
- $rk$: a ratio dividing the character number of a word by number of keystrokes with the help of an input method. The value of $rk$ varies from language to language. For Chinese, in this paper, we choose simply $rk = 2$ to guarantee that MinKSR is indeed a lower bound.

Then we can count the three sufficient statistics in Eq. 1 as follows:

(1) The count of minimum keystrokes using a general input method without the MT system:

$$mk_{norm}(t_1^m) = \sum_{i=0}^{m}(mkw_{norm}(t_i) + sn + kc) - sn \qquad (2)$$

where $mkw_{norm}(t_i)$ denotes the minimum keystrokes of word $t_i$ using a general input method:

$$mkw_{norm}(t_i) = len(t_i) \times rk \qquad (3)$$

where $len(t_i)$ is the character number of $t_i$.

(2) The count of empirical keystrokes using the MT-based input method with the MT system:

$$ek(Q, t_1^m) = \min_{cp_1^q \in CP(t_1^m)} \left\{ \sum_{i=1}^{q}(ek(Q, cp_i) + sn) - sn \right\} \qquad (4)$$

where $CP(t_1^m)$ denotes the set of all partitions, each of which breaks the human translation $t_1^m$ into non-empty contiguous sub-sequences, $cp$ denotes a specific partition member of set $CP(t_1^m)$, $q$ refers to the number of sub-sequences in $cp$, $ek(Q, cp_i)$ denotes the empirical keystrokes to input the sub-sequence $cp_i$. Let $P$ denote to the n-gram prediction list, then, $ek(Q, cp_i)$ can be defined as:

$$ek(Q, cp_i) = \begin{cases} kc & cp_i \in P \\ len(t_i) + kc & cp_i \notin P, cp_i \in Q \\ mkw_{norm}(cp_i) + kc & cp_i \notin P, cp_i \notin Q \end{cases} \qquad (5)$$

(3) Given the maximum length of n-gram prediction list $W$, the count of minimum idealized keystrokes using the MT-based input method with the aid of the perfect MT candidate $t_1^m$:

$$pk(t_1^m) = \begin{cases} \frac{m}{W} \times (kc + sn) - sn & m \bmod W = 0 \\ \lfloor \frac{m}{W} \rfloor \times (kc + sn) + kc & m \bmod W \neq 0 \end{cases} \qquad (6)$$

The default value of $W$ is 4 in this paper.

In conclusion, with the sufficient statistics above, the value of MinKSR on sentence-level can be calculated by Eq. 1. In addition, the value of MinKSR on corpus-level is given by the equation:

$$r = \frac{\sum_{t \in T} mk_{norm}(t) - \sum_{t \in T, Q \in \{Q\}} ek(Q, t)}{\sum_{t \in T} mk_{norm}(t) - \sum_{t \in T} pk(t)} \tag{7}$$

where $T$ denotes the set of translation references.

Both $pk(t_1^m)$ and $ek(Q, t_1^m)$ emphasize the n-gram matching. As a result, MinKSR is an extension to BLEU. MinKSR optimizes deep information required by the CAT-oriented input method, including n-best candidates, hypotheses, translation rules, and the perfect beginnings of the final MT results. And the BLEU scores of the final MT results don't really change.

What's more, following the Eq. 3, MinKSR can be adjusted to suit other languages by changing the value of $rk$ according to [3,5].

## 4   MinKSR with Length Penalty

We have considered the word choice and the word order in baseline MinKSR. Now we focus on the length of MT candidates. Let $c$ be the average length of the final MT candidates in the n-best list and $t$ be the reference length. Inspired by BLEU, we compute the brevity penalty BP:

$$BP = \begin{cases} 1 & if \ c \leq t \\ e^{1-\frac{c}{t}} & if \ c > t \end{cases} \tag{8}$$

Then,

$$MinKSR = BP \times r \tag{9}$$

The value of MinKSR ranges from 0 to 1. The higher the value of MinKSR is, the more the keystrokes can be saved. The *perfect* MT results for the source sentence will attain a score 1 if it is identical to the human translation.

## 5   Experiments

We conduct the experiments, including comparison tests, the correlation tests and the human productivity tests, to compare MinKSR with two popular metrics BLEU and TER. To have a comprehensive understanding, we measure the human productivity from three perspectives: translation time, keystrokes and translation quality.

### 5.1   Experimental Setup

The experiments are conducted on English-to-Chinese translation. The statistical significance test is performed by the re-sampling approach [8].

Firstly, we re-implement CoCat input method and a similar phrase-based MT system according to [7,14]. The integrated MT system is trained on about 10,000,000 parallel sentence pairs of English-Chinese news.

Secondly, in order to conduct the productivity tests, we re-implement a similar CAT platform according to [7]. This platform allows us to analyze the translation time, keystrokes and translation quality in detail afterwards.

Next, we will introduce the practitioners and experimental data of the human productivity tests:

**Professional Translation Practitioners:** Following the convention, we recruited 12 professional translators for our study. We divided the 12 translators into 4 groups evenly (A/B/C/D). Each translator translated the same set of sentences from English to Chinese. All of the professional translators are Chinese native speakers.

**Human Translation Experimental Data:** We choose 480 sentences from China news (prior to December 2014) of China Daily as the test set for human translators. This test set contains 11,869 English words. Each sentence ranges from 23 to 26 words. Then, we split the test data into 12 subsets randomly and evenly as shown in Table 1. In Table 1, each subset, including 40 sentences, for one metric. All the translators in the same groups run the exact same test.

The professional translators were asked to translate the text with four different assistant tools: (1) the Google Pinyin ("Google"); (2) the CoCat input method ("CoCat"); (3) post-editing with the Google Pinyin ("PE+Google"); (4) post-editing with the CoCat input method ("PE+CoCat"). Naturally, for each human translator, he/she should translate different sentences when using different assistant tools and evaluation metrics. And Table 2 shows the details about the permutation of assignments inspired by the previous works [6,9].

**Table 1.** The statistics of the 4 groups of human translation test subset data $M_1/M_2/M_3/M_4$. Each group of test data contains 3 subsets, and each subsets contains 40 sentences for one metric.

| English-Chinese | | | |
|---|---|---|---|
| #translators | 12 | | |
| male/female | 6/6 | | |
| Words | | | |
| | BLEU | TER | MinKSR |
| Total | 3,918 | 3,849 | 4,102 |
| $M_1$ | 990 | 1,031 | 1,058 |
| $M_2$ | 983 | 966 | 1,012 |
| $M_3$ | 969 | 980 | 1,025 |
| $M_4$ | 976 | 882 | 1,007 |

**Table 2.** The permutation of assignments for each metric. Translation subsets $M_1$–$M_4$ are assigned to the human translator groups A–D under the various assistances.

|          | A     | B     | C     | D     |
|----------|-------|-------|-------|-------|
| Google   | $M_1$ | $M_4$ | $M_3$ | $M_2$ |
| CoCat    | $M_2$ | $M_1$ | $M_4$ | $M_3$ |
| PE+Google| $M_3$ | $M_2$ | $M_1$ | $M_4$ |
| PE+CoCat | $M_4$ | $M_3$ | $M_2$ | $M_1$ |

**Table 3.** The comparison of BLEU, TER and MinKSR.

| Part | Metric          | BLEU(%) | | TER(%) | | MinKSR(%) | | Perfect Begin.(%) | |
|------|-----------------|---------|---------|---------|---------|-----------|-----------|-----------|-----------|
|      |                 | Dev     | Test    | Dev     | Test    | Dev       | Test      | Dev       | Test      |
| 1    | Baseline (BLEU) | **22.78** | **21.86** | **60.11** | **61.16** | 41.16     | 40.50     | 41.30     | 40.98     |
|      | TER             | 21.49   | 20.28   | 58.91   | 60.19   | 39.84     | 38.94     | 38.20     | 36.86     |
|      | MinKSR          | **22.62** | **21.91** | **60.17** | **61.23** | **41.37**\*\* | **40.73**\*\* | <u>48.90</u>\*\* | <u>48.52</u>\*\* |
| 2    | Baseline (BLEU) | **21.86** | **21.98** | **61.88** | **60.81** | 40.53     | 40.22     | 40.60     | 40.39     |
|      | TER             | 20.00   | 20.40   | 60.33   | 59.89   | 39.15     | 38.84     | 36.10     | 35.69     |
|      | MinKSR          | **21.59** | **22.02** | **61.49** | **60.58** | **40.75**\*\* | **40.58**\*\* | <u>49.20</u>\*\* | <u>48.73</u>\*\* |

- Part 1 and 2 are parallel experiments.
- "\*\*" means the scores are significantly better than the corresponding previous lines with $p < 0.05$.

In the real world, there are many factors which may influence our experimental results, such as the different characteristic of the translators. To exclude the translation irrelevant factors and retain consistency, we process the user data purely following [7].

## 5.2   Results and Analysis

**(1) The Comparison Tests.** To have a general understanding about MinKSR, we first compare test results with two popular metrics BLEU and TER. We choose a set of 4,040 English news sentences (56,149 words), which was translated into Chinese (81,113 characters, 36,995 words) by professional translators, from China Daily, and randomly split them into two parts, e.g., the repeated experiments "Part 1" and "Part 2" in Table 3. Each part is randomly divided into two groups: development set (Dev) including 1,000 sentence pairs, and test set (Test) including 1,020 pairs. The integrated MT system is tuned by the corresponding development set using ZMERT [15] with the objective to optimize BLEU, TER and MinKSR respectively. The corresponding systems and results are denoted as "BLEU", "TER" and "MinKSR". Then, all translation results of the development sets and test sets are evaluated with BLEU, TER and MinKSR. In addition, we count the number of sentences which have perfect beginning fragments, and the results are labeled "Perfect Begin." We report all the results in Table 3.

If we focus only on the bold figures (e.g., 22.78 vs. 22.62) in Table 3, we can find that MinKSR performs very similarly with BLEU on corpus-level evaluation while the difference between MinKSR and TER is much bigger (e.g., 22.62 vs. 21.49). And it is reasonable since both MinKSR and BLEU emphasize the n-gram matching as mentioned before. In contrast to BLEU and TER, the Figures in Table 3 show that we can increase at least 1.79 and 0.23 MinKSR scores by tuning the MT system with MinKSR on the test set. The scores show that it has the potential to reduce more keystrokes through resetting a fitting evaluation metric.

If we focus on the underline figures in Table 3, we can find that MinKSR can increase at least 7.5 and 10.7% of perfect beginning fragments over TER and BLEU. As mentioned before, perfect beginning fragments are very important to the CAT scenario. Thus, the results are very significant.

To sum up, MinKSR is an extension to BLEU, and performs very similarly to BLEU. It optimizes the intermediate MT results, such as the perfect beginning fragments, required by the CAT-oriented input method, while the BLEU scores of the final MT results don't really change.

**(2) The Correlation Tests.** We further test whether MinKSR scores are positively correlated with the practical keystroke saving ratio (PKSR) of translation process. The translators retyped 2,040 pre-translated target (Chinese) sentences of the test set under different helper settings (a total of 8 times): the Google Pinyin input method (denoted as "Google"), the pure CoCat input method without MT ("CoCat-MT"), CoCat with the MT system but n-gram prediction disabled ("CoCat(−P) + MT"), full-featured CoCat with the MT system ("CoCat(+P)+MT"). During the analysis, We report all the results in Table 4. The bold figures in Table 4 reveal that the CAT-oriented input method integrated with MinKSR increases over 1.10 and 0.44 PKSR scores compared to TER and BLEU on the test set.

The correlation tests show that there is indeed a positive correlation between the MinKSR scores and the practical keystroke savings ratio.

**(3) The Human Productivity Tests.** At last, we test the performance of three metrics on the ultimate goal of MinKSR, namely, improving the

**Table 4.** The practical keystroke savings ratio (%) based on the MT system tuned by BLEU, MinKSR and TER.

| Part | Google | CoCat-MT | CoCat(−P)+MT | | | CoCat(+P)+MT | | |
|---|---|---|---|---|---|---|---|---|
| | | | BLEU(%) | TER(%) | MinKSR(%) | BLEU(%) | TER(%) | MinKSR(%) |
| 1 | 37.40 | 33.93 | 44.20 | 43.28 | **44.67**** | 48.44 | 47.31 | **48.89**** |
| 2 | 36.44 | 35.15 | 45.24 | 44.84 | **45.64**** | 47.70 | 47.04 | **48.14**** |

- Part 1 and 2 are the repeated experimentss
- "**" means the scores are significantly better than the corresponding previous columns with $p < 0.05$.

**Table 5.** Translation time, keystrokes and translation quality.

| | Approach | A | | | B | | | C | | | D | | | Total | | |
|---|---|---|---|---|---|---|---|---|---|---|---|---|---|---|---|---|
| | | time (s) | keystrokes | quality (BLEU) | time (s) | keystrokes | quality (BLEU) | time (s) | keystrokes | quality (BLEU) | time (s) | keystrokes | quality (BLEU) | time (s) | keystrokes | quality (BLEU) |
| TER | Google | 114.68 | 209.83 | 68.17 | 110.67 | 236.78 | 72.25 | 80.39 | 168.65 | 75.96 | 100.30 | 184.30 | 71.57 | 102.38 | 204.26 | 72.12 |
| | CoCat | 89.61** | 138.41** | 73.72** | 98.05** | 168.13** | 78.15** | 68.05** | 93.94** | 83.63** | 71.56** | 124.33** | 79.64** | 84.03** | 134.85** | 78.73** |
| | PE+Google | 64.70 | 100.66 | 78.49 | 52.93 | 92.24 | 80.74 | 83.25 | 158.13 | 77.02 | 71.78 | 121.81 | 77.72 | 66.59 | 115.75 | 78.79 |
| | PE+CoCat | 52.03** | 59.36** | 81.53** | 48.34** | 63.44** | 85.32** | 65.43** | 80.77** | 82.43** | 66.90** | 82.11** | 72.76 | 56.63** | 69.87** | 81.98** |
| BLEU | Google | 101.48 | 198.72 | 69.55 | 94.67 | 221.68 | 74.64 | 76.45 | 148.44 | 77.12 | 91.45 | 160.75 | 73.26 | 91.32 | 182.74 | 73.53 |
| | CoCat | 76.20** | 124.30** | 76.27** | 78.80** | 154.62** | 81.77** | 61.96** | 75.91** | 85.65** | 62.41** | 103.51** | 82.38** | 69.96** | 114.35** | 81.29** |
| | PE+Google | 68.32 | 104.85 | 77.54 | 58.22 | 96.24 | 81.75 | 88.92 | 163.33 | 75.72 | 74.78 | 131.84 | 74.42 | 72.74 | 124.25 | 77.31 |
| | PE+CoCat | 51.39** | 57.85** | 82.36** | 50.23** | 62.73** | 85.72** | 50.02** | 78.99** | 83.09** | 68.94** | 84.71** | 79.35 | 55.09** | 71.24** | 82.63** |
| Min-KSR | Google | 109.74 | 204.32 | 68.72 | 102.83 | 229.98 | 73.93 | 78.44 | 161.83 | 76.81 | 101.49 | 164.84 | 72.02 | 98.42 | 191.55 | 72.66 |
| | CoCat | 75.08** | 120.89** | 77.80** | 76.24** | 143.42** | 81.24** | 60.44** | 82.91** | 87.01** | 66.14** | 94.30** | 80.12** | 69.48** | 110.24** | 81.76** |
| | PE+Google | 66.28 | 102.65 | 77.91 | 55.85 | 95.91 | 82.12 | 85.78 | 160.16 | 75.98 | 72.43 | 125.76 | 76.72 | 70.43 | 121.74 | 78.71 |
| | PE+CoCat | 46.62** | 52.49** | 84.52** | 46.96** | 60.00** | 87.03** | 61.34** | 77.58** | 84.58** | 63.80** | 75.56** | 83.51 | 54.23** | 66.48** | 84.32** |

"**" means the scores are significantly better than the corresponding previous lines with $p < 0.01$.

productivity of human translators. We analyze the human productivity in terms of translation time, keystrokes and translation quality. To improve the robustness, we average the result values of repeated measurements. All the results are reported in Table 5. To improve clarity, the comparison statistics of translation time, keystrokes and translation quality over various assistance are reported in Fig. 3. As we can see in Fig. 3, on average, human translators are faster and also achieve better translation quality using CoCat with MinKSR (translating from scratch or post-editing). Thus, the results in Table 5 verified further the feasibility of the MinKSR evaluation metric and the CAT-oriented input method.

For translation time and keystrokes, the underline figures and the bold figures in Table 5 show that our proposed MinKSR always helps human translators using CoCat input method significantly (with $p < 0.01$), saving more than 1.59 % time and over 4.85 % keystrokes compared with the strong baseline, i.e., (line "MinKSR PE+CoCat" vs. line "BLEU PE+CoCat" and line "MinKSR PE+CoCat" vs. line "TER PE+CoCat").

For translation quality, the figures in Table 5 demonstrate that MinKSR can help human translators using the CoCat input method improve the translation quality significantly as well (with $p < 0.01$) by more than 1.6 absolute BLEU scores over the strong baseline, i.e., (line "MinKSR PE+CoCat" vs. line "BLEU PE+CoCat").

In short, the human productivity tests establish that MinKSR improves actually the productivity of human translations using the CAT-oriented input method.

In summary, the results of all the above experiments are very promising. Under the guidance of MinKSR, the underlying MT generates more useful deep information for the CAT-oriented input method. In the CAT scenario, MinKSR helps the input method reduce substantially and firmly the keystrokes of translating process for coordinating human translators, and significantly improves the actual productivity of human translations.

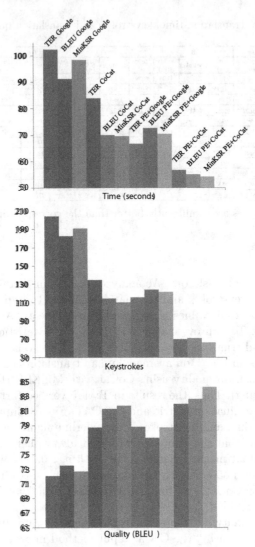

**Fig. 3.** The comparisons of translation time (seconds), keystrokes and quality (BLEU).

## 6   Conclusion

In this paper, we proposed the MinKSR evaluation metric for coordinating human translators with the CAT-oriented input method. MinKSR evaluates both the final MT results and the intermediate results (e.g., n-best candidates, hypotheses and translation rules), and estimates the keystrokes that can be saved at least by the integrated MT system. MinKSR is an extension to BLEU. Under the guidance of MinKSR, the MT system generates more useful deep information for the input method. Experiments have shown that MinKSR helps the CAT-oriented input method substantially reduce the keystrokes of translation process, and significantly improve the productivity of human translation. Further more, MinKSR has been friendly combined with the input method, the existing MT system and the CAT platform.

**Acknowledgments.** The research work has been partially funded by the Natural Science Foundation of China (NSFC) under Grant No. 61403379 and No. 61402123.

# References

1. Barrachina, S., Bender, O., Casacuberta, F., Cubel, J.C.E., Khadivi, S., Lagarda, A., Ney, H., Jesus Tomas, E.V., Vilar, J.: Statistical approaches to computer-assisted translation. Comput. Linguist. **35**(1), 3–28 (2009)
2. Carl, M., Dragsted, B., Elming, J., Hardt, D., Jakobsen, A.L.: The process of post-editing: a pilot study. Copenhagen Stud. Lang. **41**, 131–142 (2011)
3. Cui, W.: Evaluation of chinese character keyboards. IEEE Comput. **18**(1), 54–59 (1985)
4. Foster, G.: Text prediction for translators. Université de Montréal (2002)
5. Garay-Vitoria, N., Abascal, J.: Text prediction systems: a survey. Univ. Access Inf. Soc. **4**(3), 188–203 (2006)
6. Green, S., Wang, S.I., Chuang, J., Heer, J., Schuster, S., Manning, C.D.: Human effort and machine learnability in computer aided translation. In: Proceedings of the EMNLP 2014 (2014)
7. Huang, G., Zhang, J., Zhou, Y., Zong, C.: A new input method for human translators: integrating machine translation effectively and imperceptibly. In: Proceedings of the IJCAI 2015 (2015)
8. Koehn, P.: Statistical significance tests for machine translation evaluation. In: Proceedings of the EMNLP 2004 (2004)
9. Koehn, P.: A process study of computer-aided transltion. Mach. Transl. J. **23**(4), 241–263 (2009)
10. Koehn, P.: Computer-aided translation. Machine Translation Marathon (2012)
11. Och, F.J., Zens, R., Ney, H.: Efficient search for interactive statistical machine translation. In: Proceedings of EACL 2003 (2003)
12. Papineni, K., Roukos, S., Ward, T., Zhu, W.: Bleu: a method for automatic evaluation of machine translation. In: Proceedings of the ACL 2002 (2002)
13. Snover, M., JDorr, B., Schwartz, R., Micciulla, L., Makhoul, J.: A study of translation edit rate with targeted human annotation. In: Conference of the Association for Machine Translation in the Americas (2006)
14. Xiong, D., Liu, Q., Lin, S.: Maximum entropy based phrase reordering model for statistical machine translation. In: Proceedings of COLING-ACL 2006 (2006)
15. Zaidan, O.F.: Z-mert: a fully configurable open source tool for minimum error rate training of machine translation systems. Prague Bull. Math. Linguist. **91**, 79–88 (2009)
16. Zhechev, V.: Machine translation infrastructure and post-ediing performance at autodesk. In: AMTA 2012 Workshop on Post-Editing Technology and Practice (2012)

# Pivot-Based Semantic Splicing for Neural Machine Translation

Di Liu, Conghui Zhu[✉], Tiejun Zhao, Xiaoxue Wang,
and Muyun Yang

Harbin Institute of Technology, Harbin 150001, China
{Liudi, chzhu, tjzhao, wangxiaoxue, ymy}@mtlab.hit.edu.cn

**Abstract.** Current neural machine translation (NMT) usually extracts a fixed-length semantic representation for source sentence, and then depends on this representation to generate corresponding target translation. In this paper, we proposed a pivot-based semantic splicing model (PBSSM) to obtain a semantic representation including more translation information for source sentence, thus improving the translation performance of NMT. The spliced semantic representation is derived from source languages of trilingual parallel corpus by the pivot-based NMT. Besides, the proposed PBSSM only depends on one source language to generate its semantic representation during the encoding process. We integrated it into the NMT architecture. Experiments on the English-Japanese translation task show that our model achieves a substantial improvement by up to 22.9% (3.74 BLEU) over the baseline.

**Keywords:** Neural machine translation · Pivot-based translation · Semantic splicing

## 1 Introduction

The neural machine translation systems implemented as encoder-decoder network with recurrent neural networks (Mikolov et al. 2010; Rumelhart et al. 1988; Sundermeyer et al. 2012) have achieved impressive performance in many translation tasks (Sutskever et al. 2014; Cho et al. 2014a). Current neural machine translation (NMT) methods usually extract a fixed-length semantic representation for source sentence, and then generate corresponding target translation depending on the representation (Sutskever et al. 2014). Obviously, the semantic representation obtained by the encoder is essential to NMT.

In order to obtain more effective semantic vector, many researchers use multilingual parallel corpus to train a system that consists multiple encoders and multiple decoders (Luong et al. 2015a; Dong et al. 2015; Ando and Zhang 2004; Cohn et al. 2007). Despite their success, these methods center around learning semantic representation depending on multilingual input to the encoder. However, they neglect the equivalent translation information between multilingual inputs. This work shows that the equivalent translation information is beneficial for NMT.

In this paper, we put forward the pivot-based NMT model, which significantly improves the translation quality of English to Japanese. Based on the pivot-based NMT model, we further enrich the semantic representation, proposing a pivot-based semantic

© Springer Nature Singapore Pte Ltd. 2016
M. Yang and S. Liu (Eds.): CWMT 2016, CCIS 668, pp. 14–24, 2016.
DOI: 10.1007/978-981-10-3635-4_2

splicing model (PBSSM) that achieves a substantial improvement of up to 3.74 BLEU points over the baseline.

## 2  Background

In this section, we mainly introduce the pivot-based translation and NMT model with attention mechanism: RNN-Search (Bahdanau et al. 2015). On the basis of these work, we put forward pivot-based NMT model and its semantic splicing extension model (PBSSM).

### 2.1  Pivot-Based Machine Translation

When being lack of the bilingual parallel corpus from the source language to the target language, the whole translation performance will be degraded. To solve the problem caused by the lack of parallel corpus, the pivot language is introduced. The pivot language as an intermediary establishes a bridge from the source language to the target language. Pivot-based translation model is shown in Fig. 1.

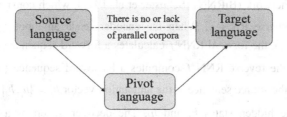

**Fig. 1.** The Pivot-based translation architecture

The representative research methods of pivot-based translation can be divided into phrase-based translation method (Cohn et al. 2007), sentence-based translation method (Utiyama et al. 2007) and Corpus-based method (Hua et al. 2009). At present, the research on pivot-based translation is mainly carried out in Statistics Machine Translation (SMT). Inspired by the success of NMT, we implement the pivot-based machine translation by neural network, and propose pivot-based NMT model.

### 2.2  Attention-Based Neural Machine Translation

The basic NMT model consists of an encoder and a decoder. The encoder reads and encodes a source sentence, a sequence of vectors $x = (x1, x2, \ldots, x_m)$, into a semantic representation $C$. The decoder then generates one target word $y_j$, $(1 \leq j \leq n)$ at a time from the encoded semantic representation $c$. Motivated from the observation in (Cho et al. 2014a), Bahdanau adopted attention mechanism in NMT model, proposed the attention-based neural machine translation model (Bahdanau et al. 2015) (Fig. 2).

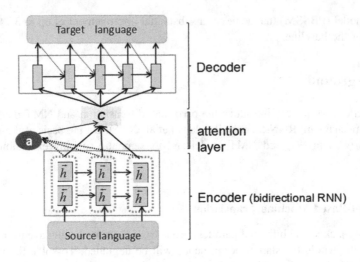

**Fig. 2.** The attention-based NMT model

The attention mechanism in translation task allows the model to learn to align words when translating. The encoder of this model is constructed by a bidirectional recurrent neural network (BiRNN) (Schuster et al. 1997), which consists of a forward RNN $\vec{f}$ and a reverse RNN $\overleftarrow{f}$. When the encoder reads an input source sentence $x = (x_1, x_2, \ldots, x_m)$, the forward RNN $\vec{f}$ calculates a forward sequence of hidden states $(\vec{h}_1, \ldots \vec{h}_m)$, and the reverse RNN $\overleftarrow{f}$ computes a backward sequence $(\overleftarrow{h}_1, \ldots \overleftarrow{h}_m)$. At each position of the source sentence $x$, the annotation vector $h_j = [\vec{h}_j, \overleftarrow{h}_j]$ is obtained by concatenating the hidden states $\vec{h}_j$ and $\overleftarrow{h}_j$. The decoder generates a corresponding translation $y = (y_1, \ldots, y_n)$ with Beam-Search algorithm. When given the encoded semantic representation $c$ and all the previously predicted words $y = (y_1, \ldots, y_{t-1})$, the decoder uses Eq. (1) to predict the next target word $y_i$.

$$p(y_i | \{y_1, \ldots, y_i - 1\}, c) = g(y_i - 1, s_i, c_i) \tag{1}$$

Where $g$ is a nonlinear function that outputs the probability of $y_i$, and $s_i$ is the hidden state at time $i$ which computed by Eq. (2).

$$s_i = f(s_i - 1, y_i \ 1, c_i) \tag{2}$$

Where $f$ is a nonlinear function, $c_i$ is related to the hidden states of the input sentence, and is calculated by Eq. (3).

$$c_i = \sum_{j=1}^{Tx} \alpha_{ij} h_j \tag{3}$$

Where $\alpha_{ij}$ is computed by the following Eq. (4).

$$\alpha_{ij} = \frac{\exp(e_{ij})}{\sum_{k=1}^{T_x} \exp(e_{ik})} \tag{4}$$

Where $e_{ij} = a(s_i - 1, h_j)$ is an alignment model. It is used to calculate the relevance score, which measures how relevant the $j$-th encoded semantic representation of the inputs and the output at position $i$. The score is computed with the decoded hidden state $s_i$ and the $j$-th hidden state $h_j$ of the encoder. The alignment model $a$ is jointly trained with all other parameters.

## 3   The Framework of Semantic Splicing Extension

Our baseline is implemented with attention-based neural machine translation model. In order to improve the translation performance of English to Japanese, we utilize multiple parallel corpora to strengthen the representation of source sentence with the method of pivot-based translation. As illustrated in Fig. 3.

In Fig. 3, ① refers to a typical NMT structure, ② is an encoder process, ③ is a decoder process. Referred to in the red dotted line is a typical structure of pivot-based

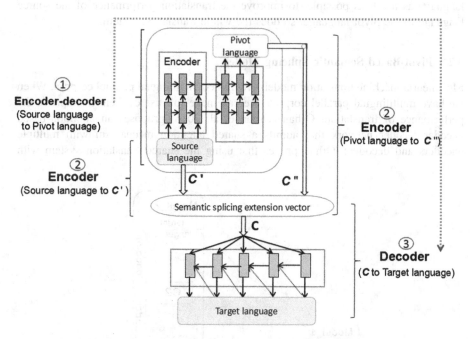

**Fig. 3.** The framework of semantic splicing extension (Color figure online)

translation, which consists of ① and ②, and ③. It is just the pivot-based NMT model we propose. In addition, to enrich the semantic representation, we put the semantic representation of the source language (② on the left side) and the pivot language (②

on the right side) together to get an extended semantic representation $C$, and then use $c$ to generate target translation with the decoder (illustrated as ③). This is the other model PBSSM (PBSSM) that we propose.

### 3.1 Pivot-Based Neural Machine Translation Model

In the case of scarcity of bilingual parallel corpora of source language and target language, the model has a poor performance (Shown in dotted lines in Fig. 1). Based on the research of pivot-based machine translation and neural machine translation, we combine their advantages to improve the translation performance.

Considering the environment of pivot language, we introduce the pivot language between the source language and the target language. Because there exist rich parallel corpora of the source language to the pivot language and the pivot language to the target language, which is crucial to the whole process of translation.

In Fig. 4, *Model*_1 and *Model*_2 adopt attention NMT model which is described in Sect. 2.2. After we finish training the two separate models, *Model*_1 can be used to translate the source language to the pivot language, and then, use *Model*_2 to translate the pivot language to the target language. *Model*_1 and *Model*_2 are two separate models, thus we try to use the available corpus of the source language to the pivot language as much as possible, to improve the translation performance of the source language to the pivot language, so does the whole translation system.

### 3.2 Pivot-Based Semantic Splicing Model

Most neural machine translation models are trained on bilingual parallel corpora. When we have multilingual parallel corpora, we can make full use of them to improve the performance of translation. Orhan (Orhan et al. 2016) proposes an attention-based encoder-decoder network that admits a shared attention mechanism with multiple encoders and decoders. Orhan proves that using the shared translation system with

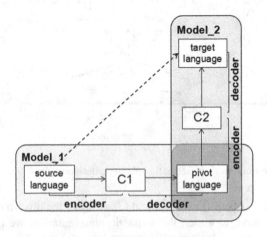

**Fig. 4.** Pivot-based NMT architecture

multiple parallel corpora can improve the system's performance with less dataset by experiments.

Some of our datasets is trilingual parallel corpora, we can use the semantic similarity between parallel corpora, and treat bilingual parallel corpus as input, which will increase the input information and extend the semantic representation. What described above is shown in Fig. 5.

To extend semantic representation, the system needs bilingual parallel corpora $lan\_src_1$ and $lan\_src_2$ as input. Using the function $\phi$ to establish a connection between the encoded vector $c'$ from $lan\_src_1$ and the other encoded vector $c''$ from $lan\_src_2$,

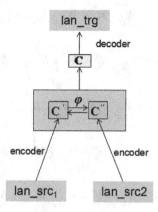

**Fig. 5.** The structure of extended semantic vector

thus we can get a new vector $c$ from function $\phi$ that represents the semantic of bilingual source language. Then, use the decoder to generate target language with $c$. As illustrated in Eq. (3), calculating the semantic representation is associated with hidden states of the encoder. When calculating the hidden states, we create the connection between the hidden state $h'$ of $lan\_src_1$ and the other hidden state $h''$ of the $lan\_src_2$, as displayed in Eq. (5) to Eq. (10), where

$$h' = (h'_0, h'_1, \ldots, h'_T), \ h'' = (h''_0, h''_1, \ldots, h''_T).$$

where

$$h'_i = [\overrightarrow{h'^T_i}; \overleftarrow{h'^T_i}]^T, 0 \leq i \leq T_{x'};$$

$$h''_i = [\overrightarrow{h''^T_i}; \overleftarrow{h''^T_i}]^T, 0 \leq i \leq T_{x''}.$$

Before the forward hidden states are calculated by the forward RNN, they are randomly initialized with $\overset{l}{h'_0}$; Calculating $\overset{l}{h'_i}, 1 \leq i \leq T_{x'}$ with Eq. (9); Initializing $\overset{l}{h''_0}$

with Eq. (6); Computing $h_i''$, $1 \leq i \leq T_{x''}$ with Eq. (10). And, before the hidden states are calculated by the reverse RNN, they are randomly initialized with $\overset{S}{h_{T_{x''}}''}$, Calculating $\overset{S}{h_i''}$, $1 \leq i \leq T_{x'} - 1$ with Eq. (8); Initializing $\overset{S}{h_{T_{x'}}'}$ with Eq. (5); Computing $\overset{S}{h_i'}$ $1 \leq i \leq T_{x'} - 1$ with Eq. (7).

$$\overset{s}{h_{T_{x'}}'} = \sigma(W_{h'x'})x_{T_{x'}}' + W_{h''h'} \overset{s}{h_{T_0}''} + b_{h'} \tag{5}$$

$$\overset{I}{h_0''} = \sigma(W_{h''x''})\overset{''}{x_0} + W_{h'h''} \overset{S}{h_{T_{x''}}''} + b_{h''} \tag{6}$$

$$\overset{S}{h_i'} = \sigma(W_{h''x''})x_i'' + W_{h''h''} \overset{S}{h_{i+1}''} + b_{h''} \tag{7}$$

$$\overset{S}{h_i''} = \sigma(W_{h''x''})x_i'' + W_{h''h''} \overset{S}{h_{i+1}''} b_{h''} \tag{8}$$

$$\overset{I}{h_i''} = \sigma(W_{h''x''})x_i'' + W_{h''h''} \overset{I}{h_{i-1}''} + b_{h''} \tag{9}$$

$$\overset{I}{h_i''} = \sigma(W_{h''x''})x_i'' + W_{h''h''} \overset{I}{h_{i-1}''} + b_{h''} \tag{10}$$

where

$x_0'$:  the first word of *lan_src*$_1$;

$x_0''$:  the first word of *lan_src*$_2$;

$h_T'$:  the hidden state of the last word of hidden state $h'$ from *lan_src*$_1$, which is the last component of $h', h' = (h_0', h_1', \ldots, h_T')$;

$h_0''$:  the component of the zeroth word of the hidden state $h''$ from *lan_src*$_1$;

$h_T''$:  the hidden state of the last word of hidden state $h''$ from *lan_src*$_2$, which is the last component of $h'', h'' = (h_0'', h_1'', \ldots, h_T'')$;

$\sigma$:  non-liner function, generally Sigmoid function or Tanh function;

$w$:  the corresponding weight matrix;

$b$:  the corresponding bias vector.

It can be known that the semantic representation $c$ contains the source information of *lan_src*$_1$ and *lan_src*$_2$ through the analysis of Fig. 5. Therefore, the target language generated by the decoder with $c$ will be more accurate. But, it is not difficult to find that the translation model of *lan_src*$_1$ to *lan_trg* and the other translation model of *lan_src*$_2$ to *lan_trg* are not independent, so do the parameters. And both of the processes of training and testing will need the parallel languages as input. It has a larger price and does not conform to the user's habits. Considering the pivot-based NMT model described in Sect. 3.1, we can extend the semantic representation based on this model,

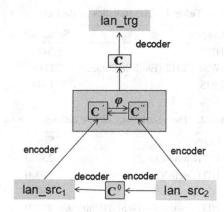

**Fig. 6.** Pivot-based semantic splicing model

which leads to the PBSSM defined in Fig. 6. Importantly, this model needs bilingual input in training while only monolingual input in testing.

The model with framework shown in Fig. 5 has a disadvantage of requiring bilingual input both training and testing. We can use the advantage of the pivot-based NMT model to make up for this shortcoming. The model we propose is shown in Fig. 6, pivot language is $lan\_src_1$, source language is $lan\_src_2$, target language is $lan\_trg$. To enrich semantic representation of pivot language, we still link it with the semantic representation of source language. Therefore, the PBSSM we proposed needs bilingual input in training while only monolingual input in testing.

## 4    Experiment

In this section, we will first introduce our datasets, parameter settings and experimental results, and then we analyze the results.

### 4.1    Datasets

We evaluate the proposed model on the task of English-Japanese translations, using more than one parallel corpus. The Trilingual corpus of Chinese, Japanese and English we use in experiment is from Harbin Institute of Technology (HIT) (Yang et al. 2006). HIT corpus contains sports, tourism, transportation, catering, and business and other fields, a totality of 59, 600 pairs of parallel sentences.

In addition, we also use the IWSLT2012 English-Chinese parallel corpus that is oral language corpus, a totality of 72,575 pairs of parallel sentences. Apart from this, there is also Foreign Broadcast Information Service (FBIS) parallel corpus. FBIS is a corpus in the news field, contains about 220, 000 pairs of parallel sentences. Table 1 is the statistics of the scale of the datasets used in the experiment.

**Table 1.** The statistics of datasets

| Corpus | Scale(pair) |
|---|---|
| HIT | 57600 |
| IWSLT2012 (English-Chinese) | 72575 |
| FBIS | 221348 |

**Table 2.** The vocabulary size of different corpus

| Corpus | Size |
|---|---|
| HIT(Chinese) | 23000 |
| HIT(English) | 18000 |
| HIT(Japanese) | 16000 |
| HIT(Chinese) + IWSLT(Chinese) | 28000 |
| HIT(English) + IWSLT(English) | 21000 |
| HIT(Chinese) + FBIS(Chinese) | 30000 |
| HIT(English) + FBIS(English) | 30000 |

## 4.2 Settings

As a baseline, we use the RNN-search model proposed by (Bahdanau et al. 2015). Since our datasets are basically spoken language, involving much shorter sentences, thus we use sentences of length up to 30 symbols. Both of the encoder and decoder have 1500 cells and 1500 dimensional word embeddings. We train each model using stochastic gradient descent (SGD) with Adam (Kingma and Ba 2015) as an adaptive learning rate algorithm. Each SGD update is computed using a minibatch batch of 80 examples. And, we use the beam-search with beam-width 10 to (approximately) find a translation of maximum log-probability. The vocabulary size of each language is set differently by experiments, shown in Table 2. Our baseline only uses HIT corpus, we trained English-Japanese model and Chinese-Japanese model separately. And, we use HIT corpus, IWSLT2012 corpus and FBIS to train pivot-based NMT model and PBSSM with translation English to Japanese task.

## 4.3 Experimental Results

We present the translation performance measured by BLEU score in Table 3. We use the RNN-search as our baseline, and test the translation of English to Japanese and the translation of Chinese to Japanese separately with HIT corpus. As illustrated in Table 2, the Chinese to Japanese translation results clearly superior to English to Japanese. Due to, in our datasets, that the parallel corpus of English and Japanese is limited, and the parallel corpus of English and Chinese is abundant, i.e.IWSLT2012 and FBIS. Thus, we take Chinese as the pivot language, English as the source language and Japanese as the target language in pivot-based NMT model and PBSSM. Besides, in the process of translating English to Chinese, we join other corpus, such as IWSLT2012 corpus and FBIS, to improve the translation performance. According to the datasets, we set up three groups of experiments. Among them, we translate Chinese to Japanese only use HIT corpus. While there are three groups settings when translating English to Chinese, they

**Table 3.** The experimental results

| System | Dataset | BLEU(%) |
|---|---|---|
| Chinese-Japanese (RNN-Search) | HIT | 22.19 |
| English-Japanese (RNN-Search) | HIT | 16.35 |
| English-Chinese-Japanese (Pivot-based NMT model) | HIT | 14.64 |
| English-Chinese-Japanese (Pivot-based NMT model) | HIT + IWSLT | 17.06 |
| English-Chinese-Japanese (Pivot-based NMT model) | HIT + FBIS | 19.53 |
| English-Chinese-Japanese (PBSSM) | HIT | 15.53 |
| English-Chinese-Japanese (PBSSM) | HIT + IWSLT | 17.38 |
| English-Chinese-Japanese (PBSSM) | HIT + FBIS | 20.09 |

are HIT corpus, the union of HIT corpus and IWSLT2012 and the union of HIT corpus and FBIS. We set the parameters as Table 2 and described in Sect. 4.2, use the model introduced in Sect. 3, finish our experiments, the result are shown in Table 3.

### 4.4 Analysis

In Table 3, the Chinese to Japanese translation result is much better than English to Japanese in our baseline with HIT corpus. This is because the lexical and grammatical structure of Chinese and Japanese is more close than that of English and Japanese. When we only use HIT corpus to train the pivot-based NMT model, the result is worse than the baseline. It is due to the poor performance in English to Chinese translation. When we enrich the parallel corpora of English and Chinese, with the improvement of the translation quality of English to Chinese, the translation result of Chinese to Japanese is also increased. Especially using FBIS to extend the corpus of English to Chinese, English to Japanese translation quality has been greatly improved, due to the large amount of FBIS, which nicely proves the validity of the pivot-based NMT model. And when we use the PBSSM with the same settings and data as the pivot-based NMT model, the translation quality has improved further, which proves the effectiveness of our proposed method once again. It is because the PBSSM uses the extended semantic representation linked with the semantic representation of pivot language which strengthens the information of the encoded semantic representation of the input, thus brings a good experimental result, and the model only requires one language as input in practical use.

## 5 Conclusion

In this paper, we explore the pivot-based semantic splicing to improve semantic representation of source input in the end-to-end neural machine architecture. We implement the pivot-based translation method by neural network, and combine other related semantic representation to the encoder on multiple parallel corpora. Experiments on the English-Japanese translation task show that our proposed model substantially improves the translation performance.

In the future, we can try to apply more complex splicing function on PBSSM, to get better expression of inputs. In addition, we can add constraint on the encoded semantic expression of input languages.

# References

Mikolov, T., Karafiat, M., Burget, L., Cernock, J., Khudanpur, S.: Recurrent neural network based language model. In: INTERSPEECH, pp. 1045–1048 (2010)

Rumelhart, D.E., Hinton, G.E., Williams, R.J.: Learning representations by back-propagating errors. Cogn. Model. 5(3), 1 (1988)

Sundermeyer, M., Schlüter, R., Ney, H.: LSTM neural networks for language modeling. Interspeech. (2012)

Sutskever, I., Vinyals, O., Le, Q.V.: Sequence to sequence learning with neural networks. In: NIPS (2014)

Cho, K., van Merrienboer, B., Bahdanau, D., Bengio, Y.: On the properties of neural machine translation: Encoder – Decoder approaches. In: Eighth Workshop on Syntax, Semantics and Structure in Statistical Translation, October 2014a

Luong, M.-T., Le, Q.V., Sutskever, I., Vinyals, O., Kaiser, L.: Multi-task sequence to sequence learning (2015a). arXiv preprint arXiv:1511.06114

Daxiang Dong, Hua Wu, Wei He, Dianhai Yu, and Haifeng Wang. 2015. Multi-task learning for multiple language translation. ACL

Cho, K., Van Merriënboer, B., Gulcehre, C., et al.: Learning phrase representations using RNN encoder-decoder for statistical machine translation. arXiv preprint:1406.1078 (2014)

Ando, R.K., Zhang, T.: A framework for Learning Predictive Structures from Multiple Tasks and Unlabeled Data. Technical report RC23462, IBM T.J. Watson Research Center (2004)

Cohn, T., Lapata, M.: Machine translation by triangulation: Making effective use of multi-parallel corpora. In: Proceedings ACL (2007)

Hua, W., Wang, H.: Revisiting pivot language approach for machine translation. In: Proceedings of the Joint Conference of the 47th Annual Meeting of the ACL and the 4th International Joint Conference on Natural Language Processing of the AFNLP, vol. 1. Association for Computational Linguistics (2009)

Bahdanau, D., Cho, K., Bengio, Y.: Neural machine translation by jointly learning to align and translate. In: ICLR (2015)

Utiyama, M., Isahara, H.: A Comparison of Pivot Methods for Phrase-Based Statistical Machine Translation. HLT-NAACL (2007)

Schuster, M., Paliwal, K.K.: Bidirectional recurrent neural networks. IEEE Trans. Signal Process. 45(11), 2673–2681 (1997)

Boulanger-Lewandowski, N., Bengio, Y., Vincent, P.: Audio Chord Recognition with Recurrent Neural Networks. ISMIR (2013)

Orhan, F., Cho, K., Bengio, Y.: Multi-way, multilingual neural machine translation with a shared attention mechanism (2016). arXiv preprint arXiv:1601.01-073

Yang, M., Jiang, H., Zhao, T., Li, S.: Construct Trilingual Parallel Corpus on Demand. In: Huo, Q., Ma, B., Chng, E.-S., Li, H. (eds.) ISCSLP 2006. LNCS (LNAI), vol. 4274, pp. 760–767. Springer, Heidelberg (2006). doi:10.1007/11939993_76

Kingma, D., Ba, J.: Adam: a method for stochastic optimization. In: The International Conference on Learning Representations (ICLR) (2015)

# Re-ranking for Bilingual Lexicon Extraction with Bi-directional Linear Transformation from Comparable Corpora

Chunyue Zhang and Tiejun Zhao[✉]

School of Computer Science and Technology,
Harbin Institute of Technology, Harbin, China
cyzhang@mtlab.hit.edu.cn, tjzhao@hit.edu.cn

**Abstract.** Recently a simple linear transformation with word embedding has been found to be highly effective to extract a bilingual lexicon from comparable corpora. However, the assumption that the pairs of bilingual word embedding for training this transformation satisfy a linear relationship automatically actually cant be guaranteed absolutely in practice. So the transformation of the source language to the target one is not consistent with the one of the target language to the source one. Given the translation candidate n-best list of a source word, we propose a bi-directional linear transformation based re-ranking method by combining the two direction linear score. The experimental results confirm that the proposed solution can achieve a significant improvement of 69% in the precision at Top-1 over the unidirectional baseline approach on the English-to-Chinese bilingual lexicon extraction task.

## 1 Introduction

Bilingual lexicons serve as an invaluable resource of knowledge in various natural language processing tasks, such as cross-lingual information retrieval [1] and machine translation [14]. Generally, bilingual lexicons can be compiled by the linguists manually or the statistical alignment on the parallel corpora. However, compiling such lexicons manually is often an expensive task, while the methods for mining the lexicons from parallel corpora are not applicable for language pairs and domains where such corpora is unavailable or missing. Therefore the automatic bilingual lexicon extraction (**BLE**) from comparable corpora [4,6,8,15], where the documents are not direct translations each other but share a topic or domain, has attracted many researchers.

In recent years, **Distributed Representation** [2,5,7,16] for a word, which is often called **word embedding**, has been extensively studied. Word embeddings project discrete words to a dense low-dimensional and continuous vector space where co-occurred words are located close to each other. Inspired by the approximate linear relation in the bilingual scenario (as shown in Fig. 1), a linear transformation [13] is learned to project semantically identical words from a language to another with the corresponding word embedding. Although its simplicity, the authors reported a high accuracy on a bilingual lexicon extraction task.

© Springer Nature Singapore Pte Ltd. 2016
M. Yang and S. Liu (Eds.): CWMT 2016, CCIS 668, pp. 25–34, 2016.
DOI: 10.1007/978-981-10-3635-4_3

In practice, the bilingual word embeddings for the words translating each other in two languages are not easy to be linearly mapped with comparable corpora. The reasons can be explained as follows:

- the word embeddings obtained in [13] are learned from the WMT11[1] parallel corpora other than comparable corpora which is often extremely asymmetrical.
- the performance achieved by the approach [13] is very high on the English to Spanish direction and very low on the English to Vietnamese direction. It shows the quality of linear relation of bilingual word embedding automatically learned is very diverse for different language pairs.
- all the word embeddings in a language are learned independently from some copora so that the relation between the corresponding word embeddings in two languages is not explicit to be guaranteed.

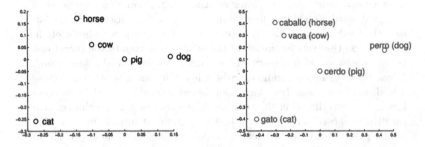

**Fig. 1.** Word embeddings of animals in English (left) and Spanish (right) in [13]. It can be seen that these concepts have similar geometric arrangements in both spaces, suggesting that it is possible to learn an accurate linear mapping from one space to another.

Under the condition where the assumption of bilingual linear relation is not adequate the transformation from the source language to the target one is very different with the one in the reverse direction. This will result in the inconsistent rank for a pair of the source target word and the correct translation candidate in the two directions. In this paper, we propose a bi-directional linear transformation (**BLT**) based re-ranking method for BLE by interpolating the two direction linear transformation scores to choose the translation candidates which both rank higher in the translation candidate n-best list. The experimental results confirm that the proposed solution can achieve a significant improvement over the unidirectional linear transformation (**ULT**) method [13]. Specifically, in this work we:

- firstly learn the word embeddings on the monolingual side of the comparable copora,
- and learn the two transformations from the source language to the target one and vice versa with a bilingual seed lexicon,

---

[1] www.statmt.org/wmt11/.

– then given a source word to be translated, we get its translation candidate n-best list and the corresponding scores with the source-to-target transformation,
– finally, for every pair of every translation in the candidate list and the source word, we calculate the score with the target-to-source transformation. And with two scores mentioned as above, we re-rank the source-to-target translation candidate list into the new translation candidate n-best list with a linear weighted interpolation.

## 2   Word Embedding

Mikolov et al. proposed a skip-gram model [12] to learn word embedding which aims at predicting the context words with a word in the central position. Mathematically, the training process maximizes the following likelihood function with a word sequence $w_1, w_2, \ldots, w_N$:

$$\frac{1}{N} \sum_{i=1}^{N} \sum_{-C \leq j \leq C} logP(w_{i+j}|w_i) \tag{1}$$

where $C$ is the length of the context in concern, and the prediction probability is given by a softmax function:

$$P(w_{i+j}|w_i) = \frac{exp(c_{w_{i+j}}^T c_{w_i})}{\sum_w exp(c_w^T c_{w_i})} \tag{2}$$

where $w$ is any word in the vocabulary, and $c_w$ is a continuous vector which denotes the **word embedding** of word $w$.

## 3   Bi-directional Linear Transformation Based Re-ranking

### 3.1   Uni-directional Linear Transformation (ULT) for BLE

Mikolov et al. [13] solved the bilingual lexicon extraction task with learning a linear transformation matrix from the source language to the target language by the multiple linear regression. Let $\boldsymbol{\Sigma} \in R^{n_1 \times d_1}$ and $\boldsymbol{\Omega} \in R^{n_2 \times d_2}$ be word embeddings space of two different vocabularies in two language where rows represent words. During the training period we choose $\boldsymbol{\Sigma}' \subset \boldsymbol{\Sigma}$ where every word in $\boldsymbol{\Sigma}'$ is translated to one other word in $\boldsymbol{\Omega}' \in \boldsymbol{\Omega}$, $\boldsymbol{\Sigma}' \in R^{n \times d_1}$ and $\boldsymbol{\Omega}' \in R^{n \times d_2}$. In other words, $\boldsymbol{\Sigma}'$ and $\boldsymbol{\Omega}'$ consist of the bilingual seed lexicon.

The objective function is as follows:

$$\hat{\mathbf{W}} = \underset{W \in R^{d_2 \times d_1}}{argmin} \sum_{i=1}^{n} \|W x_i^\top - y_i^\top\|^2 \tag{3}$$

where $x_i \in \boldsymbol{\Sigma}'$ is the word embedding of word $i$ in the source language and $x_i^\top$ is its transpose, $y_i \in \boldsymbol{\Omega}'$ is the word embedding of the translation of $x_i$,

$\hat{W}$ is called the linear transformation matrix. The solution of Eq. 3 is $\hat{W} = (\Sigma'^T\Sigma')^{-1}\Sigma'^T\Omega'$.

During the prediction period, given a new source word embedding $x$, the standard way to retrieve its translation candidate word in the target language is to return the top-n nearest neighbours (in terms of cosine similarity measure) of mapped $y^\top = \hat{W}x^\top$ from the set of word embedding of the target language, i.e. $\Omega$, that is

$$cand_{Nbest}(x) = \{y|\,\underset{y\in\Omega}{\operatorname{argmax}_N}\,score(\hat{\mathbf{W}}x^T, y^T)\} \tag{4}$$

Here, $score(a, b) = cosine(a, b)$.

## 3.2 Re-ranking for Bilingual Lexicon Extraction with Bi-directional Linear Transformation (BLT)

As discussed in the Sect. 1, the pairs of bilingual word embedding for training the linear transformation are assumed to be linearly correlated which actually can't be guaranteed very well in practice. So the transformation from the source language to the target one is very different with the one in the reverse direction. This will result in the inconsistent rank for the pair of the source target word and the correct translation candidate in the two directions. In this paper, we propose a bi-directional linear transformation based re-ranking method by interpolating the two direction linear scores to choose the candidate translation which can both rank higher in the candidate list.

Specifically, we firstly use the bilingual seed lexicon to learn the two direction transformations,

$$\hat{\mathbf{W}}_{s2t} = \underset{W\in R^{d_2\times d_1}}{\operatorname{argmin}}\sum_{i=1}^{n}\|Wx_i^\top - y_i^\top\|^2 \tag{5}$$

$$\hat{\mathbf{W}}_{t2s} = \underset{W\in R^{d_1\times d_2}}{\operatorname{argmin}}\sum_{i=1}^{n}\|Wy_i^\top - x_i^\top\|^2 \tag{6}$$

During the prediction period, given a new source word embedding $x$, we first use the $\hat{\mathbf{W}}_{s2t}$ to get the translation candidate list $cand_{Nbest}(x)$, and re-rank this candidate list as follows,

$$bi\_score(x, y) = \alpha \cdot score_{s2t}(\hat{\mathbf{W}}_{s2t}x^T, y) + \beta \cdot score_{t2s}(\hat{\mathbf{W}}_{t2s}y^T, x) \tag{7}$$

Here $y \in cand_{Nbest}(x)$, and $0 < \alpha, \beta < 1, \alpha + \beta = 1$.

## 4    Experiment and Results

### 4.1    Experimental Settings

In this paper, we carry on the bilingual lexicon extraction task in the English-to-Chinese direction. For the comparable corpora, we use the English Gigaword

Corpus (LDC2009T13) and the Chinese Gigaword Corpus (LDC2009T27). In order to align these two comparable corpora better, we select the part of the two corpus published by Xinhua News Agency which contains news articles from January 1995 to December 2008.

In the corpus preprocessing step, we performed these operations:

- For the English corpus, we tokenize the text using the scripts from www. statmt.org.
- For the Chinese corpus, we segment the text using the Stanford Chinese Word Segmenter[2].
- Duplicate sentences are removed.
- Numeric values are rewritten as a single token according to the heuristic rules.

Details of every corpus are reported in Table 1.

**Table 1.** The size of the monolingual corpora for English and Chinese. The vocabularies consist of the words that occurred at least ten times in the corpus.

|  | English | Chinese |
|---|---|---|
| Training tokens | 326 M | 346 M |
| Vocabulary size | 136 K | 205 K |

**Table 2.** The statistics of the train set, dev set and test set for BLE. The average number of the translations for a English word is more than 4.

|  | Train set | Dev set | Test set |
|---|---|---|---|
| Entries | 64692 | 2062 | 10576 |
| Words | 14413 | 500 | 2500 |
| Avg | 4.48 | 4.12 | 4.23 |

For every language, we use the same setup to train the skip-gram model. We use the word2vec toolkit[3] to learn the word embeddings. We just consider the words occurred at least 10 times, and set a context windows of 3 words to either side of the center. Other hyper-parameters follow the default software setup.

To obtain a bilingual lexicon between English-to-Chinese to train the bilingual transformation matrix, we use an in-house dictionary which consists of 55668 English words and 137420 Chinese words. We filter this dictionary with the vocabulary of monolingual corpora for English and Chinese. From the filtered dictionary, we randomly select 2500 (500) different English words and its translation as test set (dev set), and the left dictionary as the training set. Details of the train set and test set are listed in Table 2.

We make the uni-directional linear transformation as our baseline system, and evaluate the performance for our method and the baseline with the Top-N Precision and the Mean Rank Reciprocal (MRR). Here the Top-N Precision and MRR are defined as follows,

$$P_N = \frac{\sum_t m(t)}{T} \tag{8}$$

---

[2] http://nlp.stanford.edu/software/segmenter.shtml.
[3] https://code.google.com/p/word2vec.

where $T$ means the size of the test set and $t$ means some test word. If some correct translation of $t$ appears in the translation candidate n-best list, we set $m(t) = 1$.

$$MRR = \frac{1}{T} \times \sum_{i=1}^{T} \frac{1}{rank_i} \qquad (9)$$

where $rank_i$ means the highest rank of the correct translation for $i$-th word in the test set, and if there is no correct translation in the candidate list, we set $\frac{1}{rank_i} = 0$.

## 4.2   Results

In our re-ranking method, there are 3 hyper-parameters, $d, \alpha, N$, where $d$ means the dimensions of the word embeddings, and $N$ means the length of the translation candidate n-best list. And we use the dev-set to tune these hyper-parameters to achieve the best performance.

We firstly use the word2vec toolkit on each monolingual side of the comparable corpora mentioned above to learn the monolingual word embeddings for the two languages. In order to test our system effectiveness for the different dimensions of word embedding, we learn the word embeddings with the dimensions $\{200, 400, 600, 800, 1000\}$ in the two languages. Firstly we fix $\alpha = \beta = 0.5$ and $N = 100$, the performance of our **BLT** based re-ranking method and the baseline **ULT** method is shown in the Fig. 2. In the Fig. 2, the green dashed line is our re-ranking method and the black solid line is the baseline method. In the Fig. 2, for all the dimensions, our **BLT** based re-ranking method outperforms the baseline method significantly. At $d = 800$, the baseline system achieve the best performance. So in the experiments below, we all set the $d = 800$.

Next, we tune the length of translation candidate n-best list $N$ from the set $\{1, 2, 3, 4, 5, 10, 20, 30, 40, 50, 100, 150, 200\}$ on the dev set. The performance of the **BLT** based re-ranking methods is compared at the Fig. 3. From the Fig. 3, we can see the performance is increased rapidly when we increase $N$ at first, while after $N = 50$ the performance of our **BLT** based re-ranking method keeps constant almost. And in the experiments below, we set $N = 100$.

At last, we set $d = 800, N = 100$ and tune the different value $\alpha$ from the set $\{0.3, 0.4, 0.5, 0.6, 0.7, 0.8\}$. The performance for the different $\alpha$ is shown at the Fig. 4. According to the performance for the different hyperparameters on the dev set, we set $d = 800, \alpha = 0.4, N = 100$ in the experiments performed at the test set.

The performance for the **BLT** based re-ranking and the baseline system **ULT** on the test set is shown at Tables 3 and 4. From the Tables 3 and 4 we can see our **BLT** based re-ranking method can improve the baseline system significantly, and the Top-1 precision grow from 0.134 to 0.227, which is a significant improvement of 69%. The same growth can be seen at the MRR. We choose three translation examples whose translation candidates are improved by our reranking method from the dev set as Table 6. We can see the correct translation 召 回 of *recall* has

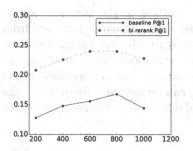

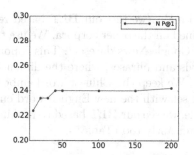

**Fig. 2.** The performance of the BLT based re-ranking and ULT with the different dimensions of the word embedding on the dev set.

**Fig. 3.** The performance of the BLT based re-ranking with the different sizes of translation candidate n-best list on the dev set.

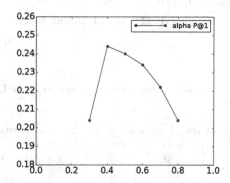

**Fig. 4.** The performance of the BLT based re-ranking with the different value for $\alpha$ on the dev set.

**Table 3.** The precision over the test set at the Top-1, Top-10 and Top-50 achieved by the BLT based re-reranking method and the ULT method.

| Method | P@1 | P@10 | P@50 |
|---|---|---|---|
| Baseline (ULT) | 0.134 | 0.328 | 0.472 |
| BLT re-ranking | **0.227** | **0.424** | **0.520** |

**Table 4.** The MRR over the test set achieved by the BLT based re-reranking method and the ULT method.

| Method | MRR |
|---|---|
| Baseline (ULT) | 0.199 |
| BLT re-ranking | **0.295** |

been reranked at the 1st in the new candidate list because the score of translated as 召回 *recall*, 0.427, is rather higher. And the wrong translation 打扰 of *beware* has been reranked lower because the score of 打扰 translated as *beware*, 0.377, is very low. For the example *netscape*, the new rank of the correct translation 网景 is better although it can't be correctly translated.

Finally, we test our **BLT** based re-ranking method on the word embedding trained on the other corpora. We use the English word embeddings released from the Google News dateset[4]. This copora consists of 100 billions tokens, 3 millions words and phrases, where the dimension for a word embedding is pretrained as 300. We keep the Chinese word embedding unchanged. The performance on the test set with the new English word embedding can be seen at Table 6. From the table, we see our **BLT** based re-ranking method outperforms the baseline system significantly too (Table 5).

**Table 5.** The precision over the test set at the Top-1, Top-10 and Top-50 achieved by the BLT based re-reranking and the ULT with the English word embedding using the GoogleNews-vector.

| Method | P@1 | P@10 | P@50 | Coverage |
|---|---|---|---|---|
| Baseline (ULT) | 0.104 | 0.262 | 0.400 | 95.2% |
| BLT re-ranking | **0.227** | **0.424** | **0.520** | 95.2% |

**Table 6.** The 3 examples whose translation is improved by the **BLT** based re-ranking methods on the dev-set.

| Examples | candidate list | rerank score | s2t score | t2s score | correct translations |
|---|---|---|---|---|---|
| recall | 召回 | 0.418 | 0.406 | 0.427 | 召回, 提醒, 记得, 罢免 回忆, 收回, 回想 |
| | 撤下 | 0.363 | 0.368 | 0.360 | |
| | 退回 | 0.360 | 0.424 | 0.318 | |
| | 扣留 | 0.352 | 0.434 | 0.298 | |
| | 开除 | 0.345 | 0.348 | 0.344 | |
| beware | 提防 | 0.470 | 0.482 | 0.465 | 提防, 注意, 当心, 小心 |
| | 当心 | 0.430 | 0.453 | 0.415 | |
| | 打扰 | 0.425 | 0.498 | 0.377 | |
| | 提醒 | 0.425 | 0.440 | 0.415 | |
| | 小心 | 0.419 | 0.485 | 0.374 | |
| netscape | 因特网 | 0.427 | 0.476 | 0.379 | 网景 |
| | 互联网 | 0.423 | 0.464 | 0.382 | |
| | 网景 | 0.412 | 0.428 | 0.395 | |
| | 浏览器 | 0.403 | 0.473 | 0.332 | |
| | 服务器 | 0.394 | 0.417 | 0.371 | |

# 5 Related Works

In the BLE task from comparable corpora, most of the previous methods [4,6, 8,15] are based on the distributional hypothesis that a word and its translation

---

[4] google GoogleNews-vectors-negative300.bin.gz.

tend to appear in similar contexts across languages. Based on this assumption, generally an unsupervised standard approach [3,11] which uses the co-occurred context words to represent the target word calculates the context similarity and then extract word translation pairs with the highest similarity.

Another unsupervised approach in [17] uses the bilingual topic distribution to represent the target word. The authors train a bilingual topic model on the document-aligned comparable corpora. It attempts to abrogate the need of seed lexicon. However, the bilingual topic representation must be learned from aligned documents.

Recently some supervised approaches have been tried to solve the BLE task. An linear classifier [9] and a Random Forest classifier [10] are used to automatically decide if two words in source language and target language are translated each other. A linear transformation matrix [13] is learned to project semantically identical words from one language to another. In this approach, the word is represented with a continues and dense vector i.e. word embedding. It is surprising that this approach achieved a high accuracy on a bilingual word translation than the standard approach. An normalized approach [18] is proposed to enhance the word embedding.

# 6    Conclusions

In this paper we argue the assumption that the pairs of bilingual word embedding for training the linear transformation for bilingual lexicon extraction satisfy a linear relationship automatically actually cant be guaranteed absolutely in practice. So the transformation of the source to the target is not consistent with the one of the target to the source. In this paper, we propose a bi-directional linear transformation based re-ranking method by weighted interpolating the two direction linear scores to choose the translation candidate which both rank higher in two the candidate lists. The experimental results confirm that the proposed solution can achieve a significant improvement over the unidirectional linear transformation. In the further, we plan to test our method on the other languages.

**Acknowledgments.** This work is supported by the project of National Natural Science Foundation of China (91520204).

# References

1. Ballesteros, L., Croft, W.B.: Phrasal translation and query expansion techniques for cross-language information retrieval. In: ACM SIGIR Forum, vol. 31, pp. 84–91. ACM (1997)
2. Bengio, Y., Courville, A., Vincent, P.: Representation learning: a review and new perspectives. IEEE Trans. Pattern Anal. Mach. Intell. **35**(8), 1798–1828 (2013)
3. Bouamor, D., Semmar, N., Zweigenbaum, P.: Context vector disambiguation for bilingual lexicon extraction from comparable corpora. ACL **2**, 759–764 (2013)

4. Chiao, Y.C., Zweigenbaum, P.: Looking for candidate translational equivalents in specialized, comparable corpora. In: Proceedings of the 19th International Conference on Computational Linguistics, vol. 2, pp. 1–5. Association for Computational Linguistics (2002)

5. Collobert, R., Weston, J., Bottou, L., Karlen, M., Kavukcuoglu, K., Kuksa, P.: Natural language processing (almost) from scratch. IEEE Trans. Pattern Anal. Mach. Intell. **12**, 2493–2537 (2011)

6. Emmanuel, M., Hazem, A.: Looking at unbalanced specialized comparable corpora for bilingual lexicon extraction. In: Proceedings of the 52nd Annual Meeting of the Association for Computational Linguistics (ACL), pp. 1284–1293 (2014)

7. Faruqui, M., Dyer, C.: Improving Vector Space Word Representations Using Multilingual Correlation. Association for Computational Linguistics (2014)

8. Fung, P., Yee, L.Y.: An IR approach for translating new words from nonparallel, comparable texts. In: Proceedings of the 17th International Conference on Computational Linguistics, vol. 1, pp. 414–420. Association for Computational Linguistics (1998)

9. Irvine, A., Callison-Burch, C.: Supervised bilingual lexicon induction with multiple monolingual signals. In: HLT-NAACL, pp. 518–523. Citeseer (2013)

10. Kontonatsios, G., Korkontzelos, I., Tsujii, J., Ananiadou, S.: Using a random forest classifier to compile bilingual dictionaries of technical terms from comparable corpora. In: Proceedings of the 14th Conference of the European Chapter of the Association for Computational Linguistics: Short Papers, vol. 2, pp. 111–116 (2014)

11. Laroche, A., Langlais, P.: Revisiting context-based projection methods for term-translation spotting in comparable corpora. In: Proceedings of the 23rd International Conference on Computational Linguistics, pp. 617–625. Association for Computational Linguistics (2010)

12. Mikolov, T., Chen, K., Corrado, G., Dean, J.: Efficient estimation of word representations in vector space (2013). arXiv preprint arXiv:1301.3781

13. Mikolov, T., Le, Q.V., Sutskever, I.: Exploiting similarities among languages for machine translation (2013). arXiv preprint arXiv:1309.4168

14. Och, F.J., Ney, H.: A systematic comparison of various statistical alignment models. IEEE Trans. Pattern Anal. Mach. Intell. **29**(1), 19–51 (2003)

15. Rapp, R.: Automatic identification of word translations from unrelated English and German corpora. In: Proceedings of the 37th Annual Meeting of the Association for Computational Linguistics on Computational Linguistics, pp. 519–526. Association for Computational Linguistics (1999)

16. Turian, J., Ratinov, L., Bengio, Y.: Word representations: a simple and general method for semi-supervised learning. In: Proceedings of the 48th Annual Meeting of the Association for Computational Linguistics, pp. 384–394. Association for Computational Linguistics (2010)

17. Vulić, I., Moens, M.F.: Detecting highly confident word translations from comparable corpora without any prior knowledge. In: Proceedings of the 13th Conference of the European Chapter of the Association for Computational Linguistics, pp. 449–459. Association for Computational Linguistics (2012)

18. Xing, C., Wang, D., Liu, C., Lin, Y.: Normalized word embedding and orthogonal transform for bilingual word translation. In: Proceedings of the 2015 Conference of the North American Chapter of the Association for Computational Linguistics: Human Language Technologies, pp. 1006–1011. Association for Computational Linguistics, Denver, May-June 2015. http://www.aclweb.org/anthology/N15-1104

# Learning Bilingual Sentence Representations for Quality Estimation of Machine Translation

Junguo Zhu, Muyun Yang[✉], Sheng Li, and Tiejun Zhao

Computer Science and Technology, Harbin Institute of Technology,
92 West Dazhi Street, Nan Gang District, Harbin 150001, China
{jgzhu,ymy}@mtlab.hit.edu.cn,
{lisheng,tjzhao}@hit.edu.cn

**Abstract.** In this paper, we propose a novel approach learning bilingual representations to predict quality estimation of machine translation. We use two bi-directional Long Short-Term Memory (LSTM) based architectures map the source sentence and target sentence to two context vector of a fixed dimensionality, then we compute the weighted cosine distance of the two vectors to estimate the translation quality of the target sentence. Our experimental results show that our model improve the performance over a baseline system with 17 features in the English-to-Spanish sentence-level quality estimation task of WMT15.

**Keywords:** Machine translation · Quality estimation · Deep learning

## 1 Introduction

Quality Estimation (QE) is an interesting topic in the field of machine translation (MT). QE system plays an remarkable role in guiding for improving the MT performance and post-editing efficiency. Different from MT evaluation, QE systems aim at predicting the translation quality of MT system outputs without any reference translations [1,15]. The first sentence-level QE shared task is established in WMT2012 [5]. Each year since then, QE is encouraged as an successive task rely on introducing new granularity levels (sentence-level/document-level/word-level/phrase-level), new language pairs, and new datasets in different domains [2–4].

Sentence-level QE, which is the most popular track in QE tasks, estimates a score for each machine translation sentence to fitting the quality score of MT outputs or ranking, such as HTER [14]. Current sentence-level QE researches focus on feature engineering. Kinds of features from source and target texts and external resources are proposed for machine learning framework such as baseline features [17] and latent semantic indexing based features [11] and word embedding features [13]. But these features, which has played a key role in the QE, is time consuming.

Recurrent neural network have shown their potential in modeling bilingual sentence, including syntactic and semantic information. For instance, neural network model [6,12,18] have been successfully explored in machine translation.

© Springer Nature Singapore Pte Ltd. 2016
M. Yang and S. Liu (Eds.): CWMT 2016, CCIS 668, pp. 35–42, 2016.
DOI: 10.1007/978-981-10-3635-4_4

In this paper, we present a novel approach learning bilingual representations to predict quality estimation of machine translation at sentence-level. In our work, we use two bi-directional Long Short-Term Memory (LSTM) architectures map the source sentence and target sentence to two context vector of a fixed dimensionality, then we compute the weighted cosine distance of the two vectors to estimate the translation quality of the target sentence. Our experimental results show that our model improve the performance over a baseline system with 17 features in the English-to-Spanish sentence-level quality estimation task of WMT15.

The remainder of this paper is organized as follows. In Sect. 2, we introduce a sentence-level representation based LSTM. In Sect. 3, we describe our approach, which combines source and target sentence-level representations by the weighted cosine distance. In Sect. 4, we report evaluation results, and conclude our paper in Sect. 5.

## 2   A Sentence-Level Representation Based LSTM

The simple recurrent neural network (RNN) for sentence representations is to find a dense and low dimensional vector by sequentially and recurrently processing each word in a sentence. However, it is generally difficult in learning the long term dependency within the sequence because of vanishing gradients problem.

To tickle with the problem, LSTM model [7–9] introduces a new structure called a memory cell (see Fig. 1). A memory cell is composed of four main elements: an input gate, a neuron with a self-recurrent connection (a connection to itself), a forget gate and an output gate.

In this section, we use LSTM model for learning the sentence embedding vectors for QE. The architecture of LSTM illustrated in We use the architecture of LSTM for the proposed sentence embedding method as follows:

$$\overrightarrow{i_t} = \sigma(\overrightarrow{W_i}\, E_x\, x_t + \overrightarrow{U_i}\, \overrightarrow{h_{t-1}} + \overrightarrow{b_i}) \tag{1}$$

$$\overrightarrow{\widetilde{C}_i} = \tanh(\overrightarrow{W_c}\, E_x\, x_t + \overrightarrow{U_c}\, \overrightarrow{h_{t-1}} + \overrightarrow{b_c}) \tag{2}$$

$$\overrightarrow{f_t} = \sigma(\overrightarrow{W_f}\, E_x\, x_t + \overrightarrow{U_f}\, \overrightarrow{h_{t-1}} + \overrightarrow{b_f}) \tag{3}$$

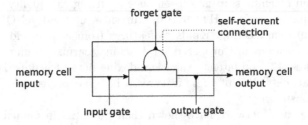

**Fig. 1.** Illustration of an LSTM memory cell.

$$\vec{C_t} = \vec{i_t} * \vec{\tilde{C_t}} + \vec{f_t} * \overrightarrow{C_{t-1}} \tag{4}$$

$$\vec{o_t} = \sigma(\overrightarrow{W_o} E_x x_t + \vec{U_o} * \overrightarrow{h_{t-1}} + \vec{V_o} \vec{C_t} + \vec{b_o}) \tag{5}$$

$$\vec{h_t} = \vec{o_t} * \tanh(\vec{C_t}) \tag{6}$$

where $x_t$ is the $t-th$ word in the given source or target sentence, code as a one-hot vector. $E_x$ is the word embedding matrix. $i_t, o_t, f_t, C_t$ are input gate, forget gate, output gate and cell state vector respectively. $\sigma()$ is the sigmoid function. $W_i, W_c, W_f, W_o \in R^{n \times m}$, $U_i, U_c, U_f, U_o \in R^{n \times n}$, $V_o \in R^{n \times 2n}$ are weights. Again, $m$ and $n$ are the word embedding dimensionality and the number of hidden units respectively.

In this paper, we use bidirectional LSTM by concatenating the forward and backward states to obtain the annotations.

$$h_t = \begin{bmatrix} \vec{h_t} \\ \overleftarrow{h_t} \end{bmatrix} \tag{7}$$

The sentence-level representation vector is computed by a single LSTM layer followed by an average pooling and a logistic regression layer.

$$ctx_x = \frac{1}{T_x} \sum_{l=1}^{T_x} (h_{tl}) \tag{8}$$

# 3   Quality Estimation Model with Neural Network

In this section, we explain our quality estimation model with neural network in detail, Fig. 2 sketches the frame work of QE with Neural network.

Let $X$ and $Y$ be a source sentence of length $T_x$ and a target sentence of length $T_y$ respectively:

$$X = (x_1, x_2, ..., x_{T_x}) \tag{9}$$

$$Y = (y_1, y_2, ..., y_{T_y}) \tag{10}$$

We represent the source and target sentences as two context vectors $ctx_x$ and $ctx_x$ by the sentence-level. And a logistics sigmoid function is used to compute the source and target QE vectors such that

$$V_x = \sigma(W_x * ctx_x) \tag{11}$$

$$V_y = \sigma(W_y * ctx_y) \tag{12}$$

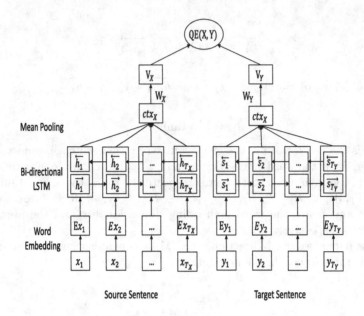

**Fig. 2.** Framework of quality estimation with neural network

where $W_x, W_y \in R^{2n \times 2n}$ are matrix weights of the source and target context vectors. The logistics sigmoid function holds the value in a range of each element of $V_X, V_Y$ in a range of $[0, 1]$.

Given a source sentence, to predict the quality estimation score as an HTER score for target sentence, a cosine distance is used as follows:

$$QE(X, Y) = 1 - cos(V_X, V_Y) \tag{13}$$

where

$$cos(V_X, V_Y) = \frac{V_X \cdot V_Y}{|V_X| * |V_Y|} \tag{14}$$

### 3.1   Pre-training with Parallel Data

Because small amount of data with does not support the training of QE model with neural network, we use a large parallel data to pre-train the model.

Given a parallel sentence pair $<X, Y>$, our goal is to maximize the negative QE score between the source and target sentences. We take the sentence pair $<X, Y>$ as a positive instance, and select another target sentence $Y'$ in sentence pair $<X', Y'>$, then package the $X, Y'$ as a negative instance $<X, Y'>$. To make the QE score of positive in larger than the negative by some margin $\eta$, we utilize the following pairwise ranking loss:

$$\mathcal{L}(X, Y) = max\{0, \eta - QE(X, Y') + QE(X, Y)\} \tag{15}$$

where $\eta = 1$, and $Y' \neq Y$ is a random translation in the bilingual data. In this paper, we introduce an additional constraints $HTER(Y', Y) > 0.7$. The model minimizes the pairwise ranking loss in all training data:

$$\mathcal{L} = \sigma_{X,Y} \mathcal{L}(X, Y) \tag{16}$$

We use the Stochastic gradient descent (SGD) algorithm with adaptive learning rate (Adadelta) [19] to learn the parameters in our proposed model. The learned neural networks are used to initialize our proposed model in fine-tune phrase.

### 3.2 Fine-Tuning with Post-editing Data

In the fine-tuning phrase, our model is trained on the post-editing data, which contains the source, target and post-edit texts $<X, Y_X, \hat{Y}>$. Our goal is to minimize the mean square error between predict QE score and HTER score, so we utilize the following loss function:

$$\mathcal{L}(X, \tilde{Y}) = (HTER(X, \tilde{Y}) - QE(X, \tilde{Y}))^2 \tag{17}$$

We also use the SGD algorithm with Adadelta to learn the parameters in our proposed model. Different from the pre-training phrase, we fix the word embedding in fine-tuning phrase. Finally, the learned model are used to predict the QE score.

## 4   Experiments

### 4.1   Experimental Settings

We present our experiments on WMT2015 Quality Estimation Share Task at sentence level of English-Spanish. We pre-train our model on the English-Spanish parallel corpus of Europarl v7 [10]. We trained bi-directional RNNs having 1000 hidden units on source and target sentence to get two context vectors of 2000 dimensions. The source and target word embedding are both 512 dimensions. The batch size of we fine-tune our model on the training set of WMT2015 QE task 1. And predict QE score on the test set in the shared task. All the data are describe in Table 1.

**Table 1.** Data settings

| Data | Size | Description |
| --- | --- | --- |
| Pre-training | 1,960,522 | Source, target |
| Fine-tuning | 13,000 | Source, MT, target |
| Test | 1,817 | Source, MT, target |

To evaluate the prediction models, we use four evaluation metrics in the task: Mean absolute Error (MAE), Root Mean Squared Error (RMSE), Spearman's correlation (Spearman), and Delta Average (DeltaAvg).

## 4.2  Results and Analysis

Tables 2 and 3 present the results of the QE models on the test for the scoring variant. We use the 17 QUEST++ baseline features to train our baseline [16]. The pre-training results are generated by our model without fine-tuning. The fine-tuning results are generated by our final model.

**Table 2.** The result on test set for the scoring variant of WMT2015 sentence-level

| System ID | MAE | RMSE |
|-----------|-------|-------|
| Baseline  | 14.82 | 19.13 |
| Pre-train | 17.26 | 23.47 |
| Fine-tune | **14.48** | **18.86** |

**Table 3.** The result on test set for the ranking variant of WMT2015 sentence-level

| System ID | DeltaAvg | Spearman |
|-----------|----------|----------|
| Baseline  | 2.16     | 0.13     |
| Pre-train | 2.08     | 0.10     |
| Fine-tune | **6.04** | **0.27** |

From Table 2, we can find that our proposed model (fine-tune) are better than baseline in both regression metrics (MAE and RMSE) and ranking metrics (DeltaAvg and Spearman). And only pre-training model have no improvement comparing with baseline model.

## 5  Conclusion

This paper described an method of learning bilingual representations to predict quality estimation of machine translation at sentence-level. This model is a language independent QE model using LSTM. We represent source and target sentences to the context vectors and connect the two vectors by consine similarity. We propose a pre-training approach to learning the model on bilingual data using a pairwise ranking loss function and then fine-tune the model on a small quality estimation data. We get a significant performance over baseline in both scoring task and ranking task of WMT15.

**Acknowledgements.** This paper is supported by the project of Natural Science Foundation of China (Grant No. 61272384 & 61402134 & 61370170).

# References

1. Blatz, J., Fitzgerald, E., Foster, G., Gandrabur, S., Goutte, C., Kulesza, A., Sanchis, A., Ueffing, N.: Confidence estimation for machine translation. In: Proceedings of the 20th International Conference on Computational Linguistics, p. 315. Association for Computational Linguistics (2004)
2. Bojar, O., Buck, C., Callison-Burch, C., Federmann, C., Haddow, B., Koehn, P., Monz, C., Post, M., Soricut, R., Specia, L.: Findings of the 2013 workshop on statistical machine translation. In: Proceedings of the Eighth Workshop on Statistical Machine Translation, pp. 1–44. Association for Computational Linguistics, Sofia, Bulgaria (2013)
3. Bojar, O., Chatterjee, R., Federmann, C., Haddow, B., Huck, M., Hokamp, C., Koehn, P., Logacheva, V., Monz, C., Negri, M., Post, M., Scarton, C., Specia, L., Turchi, M.: Findings of the 2015 workshop on statistical machine translation. In: Proceedings of the Tenth Workshop on Statistical Machine Translation, pp. 1–46. Association for Computational Linguistics, Lisbon, Portugal (2015)
4. Bojar, O., Buck, C., Federmann, C., Haddow, B., Koehn, P., Leveling, J., Monz, C., Pecina, P., Post, M., Saint-Amand, H., Soricut, R., Specia, L., Tamchyna, A.: Findings of the 2014 workshop on statistical machine translation. In: Proceedings of the Ninth Workshop on Statistical Machine Translation, pp. 12–58. Association for Computational Linguistics, Baltimore, Maryland, USA (2014)
5. Callison-Burch, C., Koehn, P., Monz, C., Post, M., Soricut, R., Specia, L.: Findings of the 2012 workshop on statistical machine translation. In: Proceedings of the Seventh Workshop on Statistical Machine Translation, pp. 10–51. Association for Computational Linguistics, Montréal, Canada (2012)
6. Bahdanau, D., Cho, K., Bengio, Y.: Neural machine translation by jointly learning to align and translate. In: ICLR 2015, pp. 1–15 (2014). http://arxiv.org/abs/1409.0473v3
7. Gers, F.A., Schmidhuber, J., Cummins, F.: Learning to forget: continual prediction with LSTM. Neural Comput. **12**(10), 2451–2471 (2000)
8. Gers, F.A., Schraudolph, N.N., Schmidhuber, J.: Learning precise timing with LSTM recurrent networks. J. Mach. Learn. Res. **3**, 115–143 (2002)
9. Hochreiter, S., Schmidhuber, J.: Long short-term memory. Neural Comput. **9**(8), 1735–1780 (1997)
10. Koehn, P.: Europarl: a parallel corpus for statistical machine translation. In: MT summit, vol. 5, pp. 79–86 (2005)
11. Langlois, D.: LORIA system for the WMT15 quality estimation shared task. In: Proceedings of the Tenth Workshop on Statistical Machine Translation, pp. 323–329. Association for Computational Linguistics, Lisbon, Portugal, September 2015
12. Luong, M.T., Pham, H., Manning, C.D.: Effective approaches to attention-based neural machine translation (2015)
13. Shah, K., Logacheva, V., Paetzold, G., Blain, F., Beck, D., Bougares, F., Specia, L.: SHEF-NN: translation quality estimation with neural networks. In: Proceedings of the Tenth Workshop on Statistical Machine Translation, pp. 342–347, no. September. Association for Computational Linguistics, September 2015
14. Snover, M., Dorr, B., Schwartz, R., Micciulla, L., Makhoul, J.: A study of translation edit rate with targeted human annotation. In: Proceedings of Association for Machine Translation in the Americas, pp. 223–231 (2006)

15. Specia, L., Cancedda, N., Dymetman, M., Turchi, M., Cristianini, N.: Estimating the sentence-level quality of machine translation systems. In: EAMT-2009: 13th Annual Conference of the European Association for Machine Translation, pp. 28–35 (2009)
16. Specia, L., Paetzold, G., Scarton, C.: Multi-level translation quality prediction with quest++. In: Proceedings of ACL-IJCNLP 2015 System Demonstrations, pp. 115–120. Association for Computational Linguistics and The Asian Federation of Natural Language Processing, Beijing, China, July 2015. http://www.aclweb.org/anthology/P15-4020
17. Specia, L., Shah, K., de Souza, J.G.C., Cohn, T., Kessler, F.B.: Quest a translation quality estimation framework. In: Proceedings of the 51st ACL: System Demonstrations, pp. 79–84 (2013)
18. Sutskever, I., Vinyals, O., Le, Q.V.: Sequence to sequence learning with neural networks. In: Advances in Neural Information Processing Systems (NIPS), pp. 3104–3112 (2014). http://papers.nips.cc/paper/5346-sequence-to-sequence-learning-with-neural
19. Zeiler, M.D.: Adadelta: an adaptive learning rate method. arXiv preprint arXiv:1212.5701 (2012)

# Research on Domain Adaptation for SMT Based on Specific Domain Knowledge

Yanqing He, Liang Ding, and Ying Li[✉]

Institute of Scientific and Technical Information of China, Beijing 10038, China
{heyq,dingliang2015,liying}@istic.ac.cn

**Abstract.** In statistical machine translation, training data usually have the characteristics of diverse sources, multiple themes, different genre, and are often not in accordance with the domain of target text to be translated, resulting in domain adaptive problem. The existing adaptive methods for statistical machine translation aim for the target text and focus on the selection of training data and the adjustment of translation models. These approaches have not specified explicit domain labels for texts or data. This study gives explicit domain labels and uses two examples for specific context knowledge, (1) Domain knowledge based on Chinese Thesaurus are applied to assign domain labels of Chinese Library Classification Number to Chinese texts; (2) Two-dimensional lexicalized domain knowledge, such as Semantic Category and Application Scenarios, is used to label Japanese sentence. Based on the obtained domain labels for development data and test data, the training data can be filtered to achieve the goal of domain consistency. Experiments show that only a part of the training data can gain a comparable translation performance to the whole training data. This shows that the method is efficient and feasible.

**Keywords:** Statistical machine translation · Training data selection · Chinese thesaurus · Chinese thesaurus · Domain label · Domain adaption

## 1 Introduction

Statistical machine translation (SMT) [1] system is usually trained on bilingual corpora (hereinafter referred to as training data), and learns translation rules from training data to generate their target translation in a log-linear optimization model. In this process, translation quality is affected by many factors, for example, the quality of sentence alignment, the scale and the domain of bilingual sentences. In general, when training data has closer domain to the test data, higher quality of sentences alignment and bigger scale of sentences pairs, more accurate translation rules will be learned and translation system will be more robust. In practice, higher quality and bigger scale of training data often results in its complex resources and diverse themes, which are usually different from the test data and lead to domain adaptive problem.

The goal of domain adaptation in SMT is filtering and devising training data, or designing and adjusting translation model, so that SMT system can generate translation results with more domain properties. There are many adaptive methods in SMT, which include data selection method, hybrid model method, semi-supervised learning method

M. Yang and S. Liu (Eds.): CWMT 2016, CCIS 668, pp. 43–60, 2016.
DOI: 10.1007/978-981-10-3635-4_5

and topic model method [2]. Data selection method design similarity functions to select the training data which domain are similar to test data; Hybrid model method divides training data into several parts, then uses each part to train translation sub-model and adjust weights for each sub-model; The semi-supervised learning method combine test sentences with its translation results to form bilingual sentence pairs and then puts them into training data to train translation system iteratively until the system acquires a stable translation performance. The topic model methods mix topic information in training or decoding process of translation system to improve translation quality. However, All above methods consider test data as a benchmark and focus on adjustment of training data or translation models for domain adaptation. Those methods have not given a clear specific domain label for their training data or test data. Once test data change, those methods need to implement domain adaptation again. If domain labels are added to each sentence in training data or test data, they can first classify various data into different special category, and then train the translation sub-model for each respective category. Thus even if test data changes, the only thing we need to do is to find domain label for test data, and choose the corresponding translation sub-model. This pattern is more suitable to maintain SMT system and helpful for data accumulation and long-term planning.

Nowadays domain has no an explicit definition. Different genres, topics, styles of language are considered as different domains; Different national or ethnic origins, dialects, etc. could be considered as different domains too. This study give explicit domain label and use two examples for specific context knowledge, (1) Domain knowledge based on "Chinese Thesaurus" [3, 4] is applied to assign domain labels of Chinese Library Classification Number (CLCN) [5] to Chinese texts. Chinese Thesaurus is China's first large-scale integrated thesaurus, which involves natural science and social science and collects all kinds of lexical resource, such as document keywords, users' query words, encyclopedias, technical terms, and all kinds of relevant professional and comprehensive thesaurus. Chinese Thesaurus contains 4 million Chinese basic words. An automatic knowledge classification system based on Chinese Thesaurus can be used for statistical classification and documents labeling so that the system can achieve CLCN-Keywords integrated operation. (2) Two-dimensional lexicalized domain knowledge, such as semantic category and application scenarios, is used to label Japanese sentence. This paper makes use of the domain knowledge to classify the data into each domain category. Based on the obtained domain labels for development data and test data, the training data can be filtered to achieve the goal of domain consistency. Experiments show that only a part of the training data can gain a comparable translation performance to the whole training data. This shows that the method is efficient and feasible. This study has an important practical value for some natural language processing task, such as machine translation, lexicon compilation and cross-language information retrieval.

The paper is organized as follows: after the introduction in Sects. 1 and 2 gives the related work about domain adaptation in SMT. Section 3 describes SMT system and its training process. Domain labeling methods and the filtering algorithms to choose the training data are explained in Sect. 4. Section 5 shows the experimental results to verify the effect on translation performance. Finally Sect. 5 is the conclusion and the future prospects.

## 2  Related Work

The domain adaptive method in SMT can be classified into four categories, data selection method, hybrid model method, semi-supervised learning method and topic model method [2]. By designing similarity functions the data selection method can select the training data which are similar to test data. TF-IDF in information retrieval is used to select the language model data [6, 7]. Lü etc. propose offline translation method to use TF-IDF to assign weight for each bilingual sentence pair in training data [8]. Matsoukas etc. use discriminate model to compute weight for training data [9]. Cross entropy and the coverage rate of words or phrases can also be found to select the language model or bilingual training data [10–12]. The differences in above methods are how to design similarity functions or which data are chosen to process.

The hybrid model methods are more suitable for online machine translation, which divide training data into several parts, then uses each part to train the translation sub-model and assign weights for each sub-model according to the context of test data. Foster and Kuhn [13] classify different sources of training data into corresponding category and assigns the weight to each translation sub-model by calculate the text distance between test data and sub-training data. The text distance not only considers TF-IDF and perplexity, but also adopts latent semantic analysis and EM technology. The online translation of Lv etc. is also a hybird model which redistributes the weights for the translation probability of each phrase table [8]. The hybrid model is also applied to word alignment to improve the translation system [14]. Koehn and Schroeder use minimum error rate training to adjust the parameters of the hybrid model [15]. Finch and Sumita trains hybrid model for different types of sentences, such as interrogative sentences and declarative sentences [16]. Foster etc. use the logistic model to assign weights for features in phrase table [17]. Baneljee etc. take advantage of the hybrid model to translate the texts from online BBS [18]. Sennrich uses perplexity minimization to adjust the parameters of the hybrid model [19]. Hal thinks that the error of the translation system mainly lie in the unknown words (OOv, Out Of Vocabulary) after transplanted into new domain, so they propose to mine the term dictionary from comparable data in target domain data to solve OOV term translation problem [20]. All above methods do not consider the topic content of test data, but focus on weights or parameters for the translation sub-model.

The semi-supervised learning method puts test sentences with its translation results into training data to re-trains translation system iteratively until the system acquires a stable performance. Ueffing and Haffari adopt semi-supervised transductive learning approach [21]. Wu and Wang etc. [22] train translation system by using the out-domain data, and then improve translation performance of system by adding translation dictionary and monolingual corpus in target domain. Schewenk [23] translate large-scale monolingual data to improve the translation system. These methods also have no specific definition of domain.

Topic models establish co-occurrence matrix for words and documents to get generative model to infer the topics. The models can cluster documents according to a given topic with a certain probability, and then automatically acquire the relationship between words. Hidden Markov models and bilingual topic model are combined to improve the accuracy of word alignment which then improves the performance of machine translation [24, 25]. Tam etc. [26] believes that bilingual Latent Semantic Analysis enables latent topic distributions to be efficiently transferred across languages by enforcing a one-to-one topic correspondence during training. They propose a cross-lingual language model and translation lexicon adaptation for SMT based on bilingual latent semantic analysis. All above methods explore topic information at word level. Su etc. utilize in-domain monolingual topic information instead of the in-domain bilingual corpora. They incorporate the topic information into translation probability estimation and establishes the relationship between the out-of-domain bilingual corpus and the in-domain monolingual corpora via topic mapping and phrase-topic distribution probability estimation from in-domain monolingual corpora [27]. Xiao etc. proposes a topic similarity model to exploit topic information at the synchronous rule level for hierarchical phrase-based translation, associates each synchronous rule with a topic distribution, and select desirable rules according to the similarity of their topic distributions with given documents [28]. Those two methods are constructed on the phrase-level topic information. Topic model methods consider topic information in texts, but their topics are automatically obtained in training on document sets, especially unsupervised learning algorithm. There are no explicit expressions of topic information.

The above adaptive methods for SMT pay more attention to data similar attributes with statistical significance between the two domains and do not give explicit domain label. This study utilizes specific domain knowledge to assign domain labels to improve the quality of SMT. This strategy combines data selection methods and topic model together and helps classify sentence according to domain labels. Thus training data are filtered to realize the adaptive goal. This study is an extend work of [29, 30] and we generalize Flow chartCLCN label based on Chinese Thesaurus, Semantic category labels and Application Scenario labels as specific domain knowledge. Once given a specific classification of domain knowledge, the domain adaptive method can be applied into any language to improve SMT.

## 3 SMT Model and Training Process

### 3.1 Phrase-Based SMT Model

Given a source sentence $S = s_1 s_2 \ldots s_L$, a log-linear model is usually used in phrase-based SMT [1, 31, 32] system to find target translation. The whole process is to search for translation sentence $T = t_1 t_2 \ldots t_K$ with the maximum probability:

$$T^* = \arg \max_T \sum_{m=1}^{M} \lambda_m h_m(S, T)$$

Where $h_m(S, T)$ is the feature function, and $\lambda_m$ is the corresponding feature weight. Our phrase-based SMT system integrates the following features: (1) Phrase posterior probability based on relative frequency; (2) Lexical phrase posterior probability; (3) N-gram language feature; (4) Word penalty; (5) Phrase penalty; (6) ME-based lexical reordering feature; (7) MSD-based reordering feature.

## 3.2    Training Process

A standard phrase-based SMT system usually includes three stages: training, tuning and decoding, as shown in Fig. 1. What need to prepare is the training data, monolingual corpus in target language, development set and test set. The training data contains bilingual sentence pairs, namely sentence alignment, from which a variety of translation rules can be extracted after preprocessing and word alignment, such as phrase translation table, MSD-based reordering probability table and maximum entropy based reordering probability table, etc. The monolingual corpus in target language is always used to train language model. In addition to various translation rules and the language model, the decoder also needs the feature weights, which is optimized in tuning process on the development set. The development set is a set of sentence in the source language, each of which is provided with one or more translation in target language. Tuning process on the development set is usually implemented by minimum error rate training, which need the decoder iteratively translate the development set by using the current weights, automatically calculate and compare the BLEU score, then change the weights until the counts of iterations reach the maximum number or translation performs become stability. This is a multi-parameter optimization problem. Based on all the obtained translation knowledge, the decoder can realize the translation process. The test set can be used to evaluate the translation performance with BLEU score.

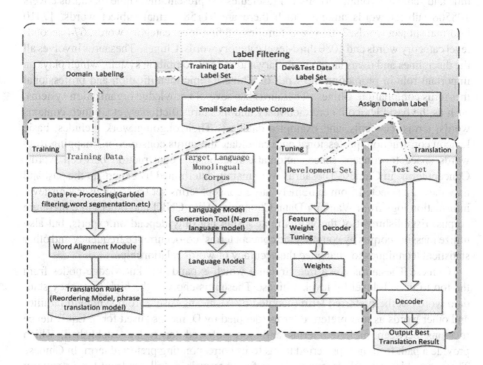

**Fig. 1.** Translation system flow chart

# 4 Training Data Selection of SMT Based on Specific Domain Knowledge

By using all kinds of concepts and classification system of specific domain knowledge this study implements training data selection of phrase-based SMT in order to achieve domain adaptation. The selection flow chart is shown in Fig. 1. Firstly, we automatically label the training data, development set and test set with domain information to get the sentence-level domain labels. Then we generate target domain label set according to both test set and development set.

Here we give two kinds of specific domain knowledge: (1) CLCN based on Chinese Thesaurus; (2) Two-dimensional lexicalized domain knowledge, such as semantic category and application scenarios. The main modules include how to label sentences with domain information and how to filter the training data. Two modules are explained as follows.

## 4.1 CLCN Labeling Based on Chinese Thesaurus

Chinese Thesaurus is a comprehensive thesaurus edited by Institute of Scientific and Technical Information of China, including social science volume、natural science volume and schedule volume, totally ten fascicules. At present, the whole thesaurus covers 108568 subject words among which there are 91158 formal subject words, 17410 informal subject words, 3707 words families, 58 first-level category words, 674 second-level category words and 1080 third-level category words. Chinese Thesaurus involves all the disciplines and owns large vocabulary and normal compiling system, which plays an important role in promoting the work of Chinese topic identification and professional thesaurus compilation. Chinese Thesaurus has several knowledge organization systems, such as the basic lexicon, core dictionary and thesaurus dictionary etc. which contains words, terms, concepts, and examples database. Their ongoing work includes: basic lexicon construction, professional core candidate thesaurus construction, mapping from words space to concept space, automatic relationship construction between words. Concept terms in Chinese Thesaurus were mainly determined by experts in the past and now they are selected from extremely large concept terms set based on user's retrieval information logs from Wanfang Data, Chongqing VIP, CNKI and other large literature corpus. Establishment of the words relationship not only depend on experts, but also utilize massive corpus by counting the concept terms' co-occurrence frequency and other statistical techniques to guarantee the accuracy of words relationships.

Chinese Thesaurus has a tree structure which expands the knowledge nodes from the top to branch level by level. Chinese Thesaurus chooses the high frequency standard words as the preferred term (denoted by Y, means "use") from synonym families and other words as non-preferred terms (denoted by D, means "used for"). Equivalence relations between preferred terms and non-preferred terms are established, which provide a path from non-preferred terms to its corresponding preferred term. In Chinese Thesaurus, hierarchical structure of a preferred term is as follows from top to bottom: the preferred term itself (Y), its English translation, CLCN, its "used for" term (D), its broader term (S), narrower term (F), related term (C), and top term (Z), respectively

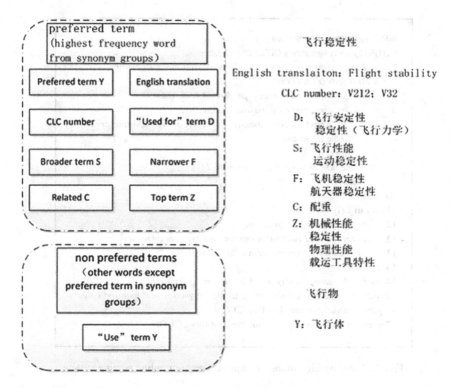

**Fig. 2.** The micro-structure of the preferred word and non-preferred word

denoted by D, S, F, C, Z. A non-preferred term in Chinese Thesaurus will be provided Y term, which is the preferred term in the family. Figure 2 shows an example of the preferred and non-preferred terms.

Figure 3 is the flow chart of Chinese thesaurus online tagging system which automatically assigns domain labels to each sentence. Firstly the Chinese sentence is segmented into word string based on the dictionary in Chinese thesaurus according to the maximum forward matching algorithm. The segmented words are divided into three types, the preferred terms, non preferred terms and words that are not in the thesaurus. For a non preferred term, its corresponding preferred term must be found. Let the words that are not in the thesaurus alone. Next for all the preferred words their frequency are counted and sorted. Then we remove the preferred terms with low frequency and find the family word for each left preferred term, merge the same family words and sum their frequency. The preferred term is sorted according to the frequency and location. The CLCNs of the first five preferred terms are chosen and merged. Finally the first three CLCNs are output as the domain label for the sentence.

We label every Chinese sentence in training data, development data and test data based on Chinese thesaurus to get each sentence's CLCN as its domain label. Thus the domain each sentence belongs to is identified approximately. For example Chinese sentence "人们从蛋白的指纹分析技术中得到启发,开发基于质谱分析的核酸指纹识别技术"

```
INPUT： unlabeled sentences
OUTPUT： each sentence's CLCN domain label
1 word segmention by maximum forward matching algorithm
2 for all words 0...n - 1 do
3        if current word is non − preferred term then
4            if contained by thesauru then
5                find its corresponding preferred term,add into array L(i)
6            else do nothing
7            end if
8        else add this preferred term to L(i)
9        end if
10 end for
11for i in L(i)
12      sort according to frequency
13      set threshold and filter out the low frequency term
13      find every preferred term's family word
14 end for
14 merge the same family word by summing frequency
15 sort preferred terms according to the frequency and location rules
16 pick words with the first five CLCN
17 merge CLC numbers, output the first three CLCN
```

**Fig. 3.** Labeling algorithms of Chinese Thesauru online tagging system

(English translation: People were inspired by protein fingerprinting analysis technology and developed the technology of nucleic acid fingerprint identification based on mass spectrometry analysis.), its output label by Chinese thesaurus online tagging system is (CLCN:Q4;Q7;T6), which means this sentence is most likely in the three sub-domain—O4 (Physics), Q7 (Molecular Biology), T6 (Reference Book). After merging all the CLCNs for development set and test set, we can get the target domain label set. Next, the training corpus is filtered according to the target domain label set and those sentence pairs are filtered out if the label of its source sentence is in the target domain label set. Thus there will be different number of sentences pairs for each CLCN. So the CLCNs are sorted according to the number of its sentences pairs. Here we also set threshold in different gradient to select training data. Finally, all the filtered-out sentence pairs in the training data are domain-consistent with the development set and test set.

### 4.2 Domain Labeling of Japanese Text Based on Semantic Category and Application Scenario

This kind of domain knowledge is borrowed from lexical analysis of Japanese nouns, and it can be generalized to any other language. Taking Japanese as an example, Japanese nouns can be labeled in two-dimensions, such as Semantic Category and Application Scenario. There are 22 labels for Semantic Category with their corresponding examples

**Table 1.** Semantic Category label set and their samples

| Japanese (English translation) | Japanese Example (English translation) | Japanese (English translation) | Japanese Example (English translation) |
|---|---|---|---|
| 人 (person) | 生徒,教師,歌手 (student, teacher, singer) | 自然物 (natural object) | 石,砂,地下水 (stone, sand, groundwater) |
| 組織・団体 (organization and group) | 政府,軍隊,国家 (government, army, country) | 場所-施設 (location-constuction) | ドア,天安門 (door, Tian'anmen) |
| 動物 (animal) | 犬,怪獣,ペット (dog, monster, pet) | 場所-施設部位 (location-constuction parts) | 窓,壁,通廊 (window, wall, corridor) |
| 植物 (vegetable) | 木,桜,藻類 (tree, sakura, algae) | 場所-自然 (location-natural) | 山,海,空 (mountain, sea, sky) |
| 動物-部位 (animal-parts) | 手,皮膚,傷 (hand, skin, wound) | 場所-機能 (location-function) | 上,边縁,境界 (above, border, state) |
| 植物-部位 (vegetable-parts) | 葉, 芽胞, 落葉 (leaf, spore, defoliation) | 場所-その他 (location-else) | 市,村,戦場 (city, village, battle) |
| 人工物-食べ物 (artifact-food) | 料理,弁当,飼料 (cooking, Bentos, fodder) | 抽象物 (abstract objects) | 理由,能力,言語 (reason, ability, language) |
| 人工物-衣類 (artifact-clothes) | セーター,シャツ,飾り (sweater, shirt, accessories) | 形・模様 (shapes and patterns) | 丸,正方形 (round, squre) |
| 人工物-乗り物 (artifact-transportation) | 車,椅子,ロケット (car, chair, rocket) | 色 (color) | 赤色,青色,黄色 (red, green, yellow) |
| 人工物-金銭 (artifact-money) | 給料,保険金,年玉 (wage, insurance, lucky money) | 数量 (quantity) | 複数,多数, 和 (plural, majority, sum) |
| 人工物-その他 (artifact-else) | 鉛筆,カップ,メガネ (pencil, cup, glasses) | 時間 (time) | 年,月,朝 (year, month, morning) |

as shown in Table 1. Some words can be assigned multiple labels. For example "fish" and "vegetables" is respectively classified as "animal" and "plant" and they also belong to "artifact-food" category. Application Scenario has 12 labels shown as Table 2. Each Japanese word can also be assigned more than one application scenario label. For example "University" has two application scenario labels as "education and learning" and "science and technology".

**Table 2.** Application Scenario label set and their examples

| Japanese (English translation) | Japanese Example (English translation) |
|---|---|
| 文化・芸術 (culture and arts) | 写真,映画,音楽 (picture, movie, music) |
| レクリエーション (recreation) | 遊園地,ゲーム,遊び playground, game, play |
| スポーツ (sports) | 選手,試合,スポーツ players, competitions, sports |
| 健康・医学 (health・medicine) | 医療,病院,患者 medical treatment, hospital, patient |
| 家庭・暮らし (family・life) | 引越し,住宅,家庭 moving house, house, family |
| 料理・食事 (cooking・food) | おやつ,食事,料理 snacks, meals, dishes |
| 交通 (transportation) | 駅,道路,運行 station, road, operation |
| 教育・学習 (education・learning) | 教授,報告,入学 professor, report, entrance |
| 科学・技術 (science・technology) | 学会,分析,理論 society, analysis, theory |
| ビジネス (business) | 販売,商品,経営 sale, merchandise, management |
| メディア (media) | 放送,新聞紙,番組 broadcast, newspaper, program |
| 政治 (politics) | 行政,政府,軍隊 administration, government, army |

When we label Japanese sentences with Semantic Category and Application Scenario, we firstly parse the sentence to get its POS tagging and then use a domain dictionary to label semantic category and application scenario for each basic Japanese word. Most of the basic labeled Japanese words are nouns and verbs. This study adopts a semi-automatic process to construct the domain dictionary by automatically generating a dictionary to represent semantic relation between each basic word and the domain keywords, then manually revising the dictionary to ensure its accuracy. Detailed construction can refer to the reference [34].

The working flow of selecting the training data in translation system according to the domain knowledge of the development or test data is shown in Fig. 1. This process is similar to the filtering process of training data in Sect. 4.1. Table 3 shows an example of labeling an Japanese term "治療薬開発 (therapeutic drug developing)".

Firstly we get semantic category and application scene labels of Japanese sentence in the training data, development set and test set. Thus each word in source Japanese sentences has two domain labels, namely Semantic Category label and Application Scenario label. After merging the two labels of each word together, combining these labels of each word in the sentence together and removing duplication labels, we got the two-dimensional domain knowledge label at phrase level or sentence level. For the example in Table 2, sentence-level domain label is "抽象物;健康・医学;人工物-食べ物;科学・技術" (abstract object; health and medicine; artifact-food; science and technology). Subsequently, we extract two-dimensional domain knowledge labels for the source

**Table 3.** An example of domain knowledge labeling in two dimensions

| Japanese sentences: 治療薬開発 | | |
|---|---|---|
| English translation: therapeutic drug developing | | |
| word segmentation | semantic category | application scenario |
| 治療 (therapeutics) | 抽象物 (abstract object) | 健康・医学 (health・medicine) |
| 薬 (drug) | 人工物-食べ物 (artifact-food) | 健康・医学 (health・medicine) |
| 開発 (developing) | 抽象物 (abstract object) | 科学・技術 (science・technology) |

sentence in development set and test set to form the target domain label set. Then two-dimensional domain knowledge labels is also obtained for source Japanese sentence in sentence pairs of training data by using the same strategy. Then we filter out sentence pairs from training data which source sentence have the same labels with the labels in the target domain label set. Thus each domain labels have different number of sentence pairs. We sort them according to the number of sentence pair and set different gradient of thresholds to select training data. All the sentence pairs in the selected training data are domain-consistent with the development set and the test set.

## 5   Experiment

The aim of our experiment is to verify the effect of the domain labeling on SMT. Here evaluation standard is the case insensitive BLEU-4 score with the shortest length penalty. The phrase based SMT system adopts Niutrans [33] developed by Natural Language Processing Laboratory of the Northeastern University of China. All the parameters are set by default and language model is 3-gram. In this study, the experiments were carried out on two respective tasks that are Chinese-English translation and Japanese-Chinese term translation.

### 5.1   Evaluation of Chinese-English Machine Translation

There are two data sets in the task of Chinese-English machine translation. One data set is selected from the experimental data of Chinese-English Patent Machine Translation Sub-task at the NTCIR-10 Workshop. The other data set is selected from Wanfang Data owned by our research group, including 500000 parallel sentence pairs as the training corpus covering different domain, as well as development set and test set which CLCN is "T" representing "industrial Technology" domain. These detailed data statistics are shown in Table 4.

Table 4.   The statistics of Chinese-English machine translation

| Data set | Data set | Language | Number of sentence | Average sentence length | Vocabulary |
|---|---|---|---|---|---|
| NTCIR-10 | Training data | Chinese | 500,000 | 36 | 18,358,889 |
|  |  | English | 500,000 | 40 | 20,460,208 |
|  | Development set | Chinese | 1,000 | 35 | 35,349 |
|  |  | English | 1,000 | 37 | 37,345 |
|  | Test set | Chinese | 1,000 | 36 | 36,492 |
|  |  | English | 1,000 | 37 | 37,584 |
| Wanfang Data | Training data | Chinese | 500,000 | 29 | 14,075,889 |
|  |  | English | 500,000 | 32 | 15,493,249 |
|  | Development set | Chinese | 2,500 | 29 | 72,830 |
|  |  | English | 2,500 | 32 | 81,597 |
|  | Test set | Chinese | 2,500 | 28 | 72,330 |
|  |  | English | 2,500 | 33 | 84,300 |

**Table 5.** Number of domain labels

| Data set | | Label number of CLCN | Total number of sentences | Number of sentences without labels |
|---|---|---|---|---|
| NTCIR data | Original training set | 1924 | 500000 | 19555 |
| | Development set | 485 | 1000 | 31 |
| | Test set | 643 | 1000 | 54 |
| Wanfang data | Original training set | 2172 | 500000 | 97571 |
| | Development set | 777 | 2500 | 58 |
| | Test set | 782 | 2500 | 65 |

The Baseline system is trained by Niutrans and BLEU score is calculated on the test set. Then Chinese Thesaurus online tagging system assign domain labels to the two data sets. Table 5 shows the number of the domain labels for NTCIR data. There are also some sentence pairs without domain labels. We take the union of the domain labels of development set and test set to get 643 domain labels and build the target domain label set. This domain label set is used to filter the original training data to get 478380 sentences pairs, which are sorted by the number of sentence pair corresponding to each domain label. Those sentence pairs with high frequency of domain label are more relevant to the domain of test corpus. This study designs gradient experiment to narrow the scale of training data and set the threshold of frequency from 0 to 8000, which means that the scale of training data reduces from 95% to 69% of the original data. By using filtered training data to re-train Niutrans, the translation performance is shown as Table 6 compared with Baseline. In the experiment of Wanfang Data, the domain of test set and development set is known as "T industrial technology" beforehand and the number of target domain labels is 796. 371229 sentence pairs are filtered out from the original training data. As shown in Table 6, our domain adaptive method on NTCIR data respectively uses 95% and 65% of the training corpus to obtain BLEU scores that are close to baseline. For Wanfang Data, when the scales of the

**Table 6.** The translation performance of translation

| Data | System | Number of training data | Development set BLEU | Test set BLEU |
|---|---|---|---|---|
| NTCIR data | Baseline | 500,000 | 0.4031 | 0.3147 |
| | Threshold = 0 | 478,380 | 0.3917 | 0.3138 |
| | Threshold = 8000 | 349,390 | 0.3906 | 0.3132 |
| Wanfang data | Baseline | 500,000 | 0.1087 | 0.1051 |
| | Training data on "T industrial technology" | 50,000 | 0.1059 | 0.1044 |
| | Domain adaptive training data | 371,229 | 0.1067 | 0.1049 |

**Table 7.** Detail statistics of Japanese-Chinese scientific and technical Term Translation

| Data set | Sentence pair/term pair | Language | Number | Average sentence length | Vocabulary |
|---|---|---|---|---|---|
| Training data | Term pair | Japanese | 4,269,254 | 10 | 44,455,737 |
| | | Chinese | 4,269,254 | 7 | 33,708,490 |
| | Sentence pair | Japanese | 1,494,874 | 43 | 65,120,202 |
| | | Chinese | 1,494,874 | 33 | 49,741,866 |
| Development set | | Japanese | 2,500 | 5 | 12788 |
| | | Chinese | 2,500 | 6 | 16349 |
| Test set | | Japanese | 2,323 | 6 | 15668 |
| | | Chinese | 2,323 | 5 | 12341 |

corpus were reduced to 10% and 74% of the original training data, the BLEU score is almost not affected, but the training time and computational complexity are greatly reduced. The two experiment results show that the domain knowledge based on Chinese Thesaurus achieves domain adaption of SMT.

## 5.2 Evaluation of Japanese-Chinese Scientific and Technical Term Translation

In the experiment, we use Japanese-Chinese bilingual corpus owned by our research group and select some sentence pairs as training data, development set and test set. The training data consists of two parts, one is bilingual term pairs, and the other is bilingual sentence pairs. The development set and test set is bilingual term pair. The detailed statistics are shown in Table. 7.

JUMAN[1] [35] is adopted in the experiment to label Japanese sentence and assign Semantic Category label and Application Scenario label to each word in the Japanese sentence. According to the method in Sect. 4.2, word-level domain labels are transformed to term-level or sentence-level domain labels. The source Japanese terms or sentences in the original training data, development set and the test set are labeled to get the semantic category labels and application scenarios labels. The statistics of the

**Table 8.** Number of the Domain labels

| Data | Number of two-dimension domain labels | Total number of sentence | Number of sentence without labels |
|---|---|---|---|
| Original training set | 144 | 5764128 | 669297 |
| Development set | 35 | 2500 | 190 |
| Test set | 36 | 2323 | 361 |

---

[1] http://nlp.ist.i.kyoto-u.ac.jp/EN/index.php?JUMAN.

**Table 9.** Translation Performance of Japanese-Chinese Sic-Tech Terms

| System | Number of sentence pair of Training data | Size of training data compared with baseline) | Test set BLEU | Translation accuracy compared with baseline |
|---|---|---|---|---|
| Baseline | 5764128 | 100% | 0.8012 | 100% |
| Filtering | 834504 | 14.5% | 0.6567 | 82% |
| Filtering relaxationI | 1421553 | 24.7% | 0.7684 | 95.9% |
| Filtering relaxationII | 2966479 | 51.46% | 0.7983 | 98.3% |

domain labels assigned to each data set are shown in Table 8. After taking union of the domain labels of development set and test set, we get 42 domain knowledge labels, and build the target domain label set. By using this label set to filter the original training data, we get 834504 sentence pairs or term pairs. They are sorted by the number of the sentence pairs corresponding to each domain label. The training data which belong to the 42 target domain labels is selected as new training data. Its size was reduced to 14.5% of the original training data, as shown in Line 3 of Table 9.

Since the filtered training data is too small and the translation performance turn worse as shown in Table 9, the filtering criteria are appropriately relaxed to conducted new training data (denoted by "Filtering RelaxationI" in Table 9). Here we merge some

**Table 10.** Rules of Filtering Relaxation

| | Labels before merging | Labels after merging |
|---|---|---|
| Filtering relaxation I | 人工物-乗り物 (artifact-rider) | 人工物 (artifact) |
| | 人工物-金銭 (artifact-money) | |
| | 人工物-衣類 (artifact-clothes) | |
| | 人工物-食べ物 (artifact-food) | |
| | 人工物-その他 (artifact-else) | |
| | 場所-施設部位 (location-constuction parts) | 場所 (location) |
| | 場所-施設 (location-constuction) | |
| | 場所-自然 (location-natural) | |
| | 場所-機能 (location-function) | |
| | 場所-その他 (location-else) | |
| Filtering relaxation II | 健康・医学 (health・medicine) | 科技 (science・technology) |
| | 科学・技術 (science・technology) | |
| | 人工物 (artifact) | 物体 (object) |
| | 自然物 (natural object) | |
| | 抽象物 (abstract object) | |
| | 动物 (animal) | 生命体 (life) |
| | 植物 (vegetable) | |

Semantic Category labels together as Table 10. For example, "人工物-その他 (artifact-else)", "人工物-金銭 (artifact-money)", "人工物-衣類 ((artifact-clothes))", "人工物-食べ物 (artifact-food)", are merged as "人工物 (artifact)". These rules of "Filtering RelaxationI" make the size of the filtered training data reduce to 24.7% of the original data., In "Filtering Relaxation II", "健康・医学 (health・medicine)", "科学・技術 (science・technology)" are merged as"科技 (science)", and "人工物 (artifact)", "自然物 (natural object)", "抽象物 (abstract object)" as "物体 (object)", "动物 (animal)", "植物 (vegetable)" as "生命体 (life)". The size of the training data is reduced to 51.46% of the original data. By using the filtered training data to re-train Niutrans, our domain adaptive method respectively reached the BLEU scores which are nearly close to Baseline score by using 24.7% and 51.46% of the original training data, and the training time and the complexity of calculation is greatly reduced. Experimental results shows that two-dimension Japanese domain knowledge can realize domain adaptive goal in SMT.

# 6   Conclusions and the Future Works

SMT often encounter inconsistent domain problems between training data and test set, which leads to worse translation performance. So domain adaptation has been a concerned research focus in SMT. This study takes advantage of factual data and topic model in domain adaptive methods of SMT and assign explicit domain label to each source sentence. Two examples of specific domain knowledge are adopted in our study: the one is CLCN domain information based on Chinese Thesaurus and the other is semantic category label and the application scenarios label. Both of the two specific domain knowledge can label the source sentences in the training data, test data or development data with domain labels, with which the training data can be filtered to achieve the goal of domain adaptation for SMT. The experimental results show that these two kinds of domain labels of sentences can help SMT system obtain comparative translation performance by using parts of the training data. Our method reduces the training and decoding cost of translation system without loss of translation performance. The strategy can be applied to any other method of domain classification. And the pattern of domain classification based on factual data, such as thesaurus or domain dictionary, can be generalized to any other language.

The study will be improved in the future. The current algorithm of domain labeling needs to be optimized and the number of domain dictionary is still sparse. Semantic knowledge in WordNet or HowNet, or mapping relation in bilingual domain is helpful to improve domain labeling.

**Acknowledgments.** This research work was partially supported by National Natural Science of China (61303152, 71503240), and ISTIC Research Foundation Projects (ZD2016-05).

# References

1. Koehn, P., Och, F.J., Marcu, D.: Statistical phrase-based translation. In: Conference of the North American Chapter of the Association for Computational Linguistics on Human Language Technology-volume, North American, pp. 127–133 (2003)
2. Lei, C., Ming, Z.: An overview of domain adaptation for statistical machine translation. Intell. Comput. Appl. **4**(6), 31–34 (2014)
3. Zeng, J., Chang, C.: Function orientation and development of new edition of chinese thesaurus under network environment. J. China Soc. Sci. Tech. Inf. **29**(6), 973–977 (2010)
4. Chinese Thesaurus. Scientific and Technical Documentation Press (1991)
5. Shunian, C.: The first electronic edition of Chinese library classification. Lib. Inf. Serv. **3**, 55–60 (2002)
6. Eck, M., Vogel, S., Waibel, A.: Low cost portability for statistical machine translation based on n-gram coverage. In: Proceedings of Mtsummit X (2005)
7. Zhao, B., Eck, M., Vogel, S.: Language model adaptation for statistical machine translation with structured query models. In: Proceedings of the 20th International Conference on Computational Linguistics, p. 411. Association for Computational Linguistics, The University of Geneva, Switzerland (2004)
8. Lü, Y., Huang, J., Liu, Q.: Improving statistical machine translation performance by training data selection and optimization. In: EMNLP-CoNLL 2007, Proceedings of the 2007 Joint Conference on Empirical Methods in Natural Language Processing and Computational Natural Language Learning, 28–30 June 2007, Prague, Czech Republic, pp. 343–350 (2007)
9. Matsoukas, S., Rosti, A., Zhang, B.: Discriminative corpus weight estimation for machine translation. In: Proceedings of the 2009 Conference on Empirical Methods in Natural Language Processing: Volume 2, vol. 2, pp. 708–717. Association for Computational Linguistics, Singapore (2009)
10. Moore, R.C., Lewis, W.: Intelligent selection of language model training data. In: ACL 2010, Proceedings of the, Meeting of the Association for Computational Linguistics, 11–16 July 2010, Uppsala, Sweden, Short Papers, pp. 220–224 (2010)
11. Axelrod, A., He, X., Gao, J.: Domain adaptation via pseudo in-domain data selection. In: Proceedings of the Conference on Empirical Methods in Natural Language Processing, pp. 355–362. Association for Computational Linguistics, Edinburgh, UK (2011)
12. Shujie, Y., Tong, X., Jingbo, Z.: Selectiion of SMT training data based on sentence pair quality and coverage. J. Chin. Inf. Process. **25**(2), 72–77 (2011)
13. Foster, G., Kuhn, R.: Mixture model adaptation for SMT. In: Proceedings of Second Workshop on Statistical Machine Translation, pp. 128–135. Association for Computational Linguistics, Prague (2007)
14. Civera, J., Juan, A.: Domain adaptation in statistical machine translation with mixture modeling. In: Proceedings of the Second workshop Statistical Machine Translation, pp. 177–180. Association for Computational Linguistics, Prague (2007)
15. Koehn, P., Schroeder, J.: Experiments in domain adaptation for statistical machine translation. In: Proceedings of the Second, Workshop on Statistical Machine Translation, pp. 224–227. Association for Computational Linguistics, Prague (2007)
16. Finch, A., Sumita, E.: Dynamic model interpolation for statistical machine translation. In: Proceedings of the Third Workshop on Statistical Machine Translation, pp. 208–215. Association for Computational Linguistics, Columbus (2008)

17. Foster, G., Goutte, C., Kuhn, R.: Discriminative instance weighting for domain adaptation in statistical machine translation. In: Proceedings of the 2010 Conference on Empirical Methods in Natural Language Processing, pp. 451–459. Association for Computational Linguistics, Cambridge (2010)
18. Banerjee, P., Naskar, S.K., Roturier, J., et al.: Domain adaptation in statistical machine translation of user-forum data using component level mixture modelling. In: Proceedings of Machine Translation Summit XIII, Xiamen, China, pp. 285–292 (2011)
19. Sennrich, R.: Perplexity minimization for translation model domain adaptation in statistical machine translation. In: Proceedings of the 13th Conference of the European Chapter of the Association for Computational Linguistics, pp. 539–549. Association for Computational Linguistics, Avignon (2012)
20. Daumé III, H., Jagarlamudi, J.: Domain adaptation for machine translation by mining unseen words. In: Proceedings of the 49th ACL: Shortpapers, pp. 407–412. Association for Computational Linguistics, Portland (2011)
21. Ueffing, N., Haffari, G., Sarkar, A.: Semi-supervised model adaptation for statistical machine translation. Mach. Transl. 21, 71–94 (2007)
22. Wu, H.,Wang, H.,Zong, C.: Domain adaptation for statistical machine translation with domain dictionary and monolingual corploa. In: Proceedings of the 22nd International Conference on Computational Linguistics (Coling 2008), pp. 993–1000. COLING 2008 Organizing Committee, Manchester (2008)
23. Schwenk, H.: Investigations on large-scale lightly supervised training for statistical machine translation. In: Proceedings of the International Workshop on Spoken Language Translation, pp. 182–189. IWSLT, Hawaii (2008)
24. Zhao, B., Xing, E.P.: BiTAM:Bilingual topic admixture models for word alignment. In: Proceedings of the COLING/ACL 2006 Main Conference Poster Sessions, pp. 969–976. Association for Computational Linguistics, Sydney (2006)
25. Zhao, B., Xing, E.P.: HM-BiTAM: Bilingual topic exploration, word alignment, and translation. In: Advances in Neural Information Processing Systems, pp. 1689–1696. Vancouver, British Columbia (2008)
26. Tam, Y.C., Lane, I., Schultz, T.: Bilingual LSA-based adaptation for statistical machine translation.Mach. Transl. 21(4), 187–207 (2007)
27. Su, J.,Wu, H., Wang, H., et al.: Translation model adaptation for statistical machine translation with monolingual topic information. In: Proceedings of Annual Meeting of the Association for Computational Linguistics: Human Language Technologies, pp. 459–468. Association for Computational Linguistics, Jeju (2012)
28. Xiao, X., Xiong, D., Zhang, M., et al.: A topic similarity model for hierarchical phrase-based translation. In: Proceedings of the 50th Annual Meeting of the Association for Computational Linguistics: Human Language Technologies, pp. 750–758. Association for Computational Linguistics, Jeju (2012)
29. Ding, L., Li, Y., He, Y., Wang, X., Zhang, Y., Yao, C.: Experimental study on training data selection of SMT based on chinese thesaurus. J. China Soc. Sci. Tech. Inf. (accepted)
30. Ding, L., Li, Y., He, Y., Liu, J.: Research on Japanese-Chinese S&T terminology translation based-on two-dimensional domain lexicalized domain knowledge. In: CWMT 2016, Urumchi, China, vol. 8, pp. 25–26 (2016)
31. Och, F.J., Ney, H.: Discriminative training and maximum entropy models for statistical machine translation. In: Meeting on Association for Computational Linguistics, pp. 295–302. Association for Computational Linguistics, Stroudsburg, USA (2002)

32. Xiong, D., Liu, Q., Lin, S.: Maximum entropy based phrase reordering model for statistical machine translation. In: Proceedings of COLING-ACL, Sydney, Australia, pp. 521–528 (2006)
33. Xiao, T., Zhu, J., Zhang, H., et al.: NiuTrans: an open source toolkit for phrase-based and syntax-based machine translation. In: ACL 2012 System Demonstrations, Jeju, Republic of Korea, pp. 19–24 (2012)
34. Hashimoto, C., Kurohashi, S.: Construction of domain dictionary for fundamental vocabulary and its application to automatic blog categorization with the dynamic estimation of unknown words' domains. J. Nat. Lang. Process. **15**(5), 73–97 (2008)
35. Kurohashi, S., Nakamura, T., Matsumoto, Y., et al.: Improvements of Japanese morphological analyzer JUMAN. In: Proceedings of The International Workshop on Sharable Natural Language, pp. 22–28 (1994)

# Automatic Construction of Domain Terminology Knowledge Base for HowNet Based on the Headword

Chuang Wu, Lin Wang$^{(\boxtimes)}$, Na Ye, Guiping Zhang,
and Dongfeng Cai

Knowledge Engineering Research Center, Shenyang Aerospace University,
Shenyang 110136, China
chuangwu2009@gmail.com, wanglin2009@163.com,
yena_l@126.com, zgp@ge-soft.com, caidf@vip.163.com

**Abstract.** HowNet is a Chinese-English Bilingual common-sense knowledge base, playing an important role in machine translation tasks. However, when facing domain-specific machine translation tasks, HowNet must be supplemented with domain-specific terminologies. In other words, we need to construct domain terminology semantic knowledge base. In this paper, we propose a method to automatically construct domain terminology knowledge base, based on the headword of a terminology. Specifically, the semantic meaning (HowNet DEF) of an unseen terminology is defined as one of the semantic meanings of the headword of the terminology. Headword disambiguation is done by considering the context of headwords and adding domain-specific disambiguation rules to the general disambiguation rules. Experiments on aviation domain show that our proposed method on headword disambiguation achieves 9.4% improvement based on the default disambiguation tools in HowNet. We also find that with our automatically constructed domain terminology knowledge base, HowNet machine translation system achieves better translation quality.

**Keywords:** Hownet · Domain terminology semantic knowledge base · Headword · Disambiguation rule

## 1 Introduction

As the resource of HowNet MT system [1], knowledge base plays an import role in translation. The HowNet knowledge base is a common-sense knowledge base, which cannot meet the requirements of the translation tasks in the specific fields (such as aviation, patent), and a large number of unknown words and terms greatly affect the quality of translation. Therefore it is necessary to construct a large-domain bilingual semantic knowledge base.

This work is supported by the Youth Growth Foundation of School(№-20141502/215108) and National Natural Science Foundation of China (№-61402299).

© Springer Nature Singapore Pte Ltd. 2016
M. Yang and S. Liu (Eds.): CWMT 2016, CCIS 668, pp. 61–74, 2016.
DOI: 10.1007/978-981-10-3635-4_6

The domain specific terms are highly professional and difficult to understand. And the existing construction methods are not only inefficient for large-scale construction, but the ambiguity of the words themselves also increased the difficulty in construction. Wang [2] proposed a method of TCM theoretical knowledge base construction for semantic retrieval, which requires additional terminological interpretation. Zhang [3] built an aviation terminology semantic knowledge base, which is manual construction. Liu [4] put forward the dynamic knowledge network model, which is oriented to 360 Chinese Wikipedia, but it still relies on manual construction. Cui [5] integration HowNet to the Wikipedia encyclopedia and used a mapping relationship between the two knowledge bases to construct a semantic annotation semantic repository. The above-mentioned methods realized the expansion of semantic knowledge in various fields, but most of them are manual and fail to disambiguate the annotations of the polysemous words.

This paper proposes an automatic headword-based construction method of the domain terminology knowledge, which efficiently improves the efficiency and quality of terminology construction. Word sense disambiguation (WSD) problems during construction are solved by taking the context of head words as features and expanding the disambiguation rules of Sense Colony Testing (SCT). We made experiments on the construction method in the field of aviation, where 500 aeronautical terms are manually evaluated. On the basis of the constructed knowledge base, 50 sentences are translated by the HowNet MT system [6] and the results are evaluated and analyzed.

In Sect. 2, the semantic knowledge base and the semantic disambiguation tools of HowNet are introduced. Section 3 introduces the automatic headword-based domain knowledge base construction method based on HowNet semantic disambiguation. Experiments and analysis are given in Sect. 4.

## 2   HowNet

### 2.1   The Knowledge Base

HowNet knowledge base [7, 8] is the core of the HowNet system which contains information like the explanation of the bilingual words, the phonetic notation of Chinese, bilingual instances, syntax, semantic relationships, etc., which has been applied to similarity calculation, words sense disambiguation, semantic analysis, machine translation and so on. For instance, there are 6 records of "plane" in HowNet knowledge base, distributed over 5 definitions. "plane|飞机", "plane|刨子", "plane|平面" are noun records, "plane|平" is adjective record, and "plane|刨" is verb record. The following samples are the two noun records of "plane" in HowNet.

```
NO.=056372
W_C=飞机
G_C=noun [fei1 ji1]
W_E=plane
G_E=noun [2 planenoun-0static 架   ]
DEF={aircraft|飞行器}
```

```
NO.=123767
W_C=刨子
G_C=noun [bao4 zi0]
E_C=一把~, 这把~不快了应该磨磨, 你会使~吗
W_E=plane
G_E=noun [3 planenoun-0   ]
DEF={tool|用具:{AlterForm|变形状:PatientValue={level|平}{polished|
光},instrument={~}}}
```

As a "plane|飞机", the DEF (also known as concept) is "{aircraft|飞行器}", and its quantifier is "架", the definition of "plane|刨子" changes to "{tool|用具: {AlterForm| 变形状: PatientValue = {level|平} {polished|光}, instrument = {~}}}".

DEF in the record provides more semantic information than the word itself. Take "plane|刨子" for example, its first feature is "AlterForm|变形状", by means of which the form of the object can be altered, and PatientValue "level|平" or "polished|光" happens to the object. Through the first sememe "tool|用具", it can be inferred that the hypernym nodes of "plane|刨子" in the HowNet Taxonomy are successively implement, artifact, inanimate, physical, thing and entity. The hypernym nodes of "plane|飞机" are successively vehicle, implement, artifact, inanimate, physical, thing and entity. The taxonomy plays a key role in WSD.

## 2.2 Sense Colony Testing

In the HowNet MT system, the WSD problems of no-syntax-related type are solved by SCT [10]. SCT calculates the concept distance of words in the given text by building relevant concept fields with Concept Inference Machine (CIM). CIM is a rule-based inference machine, which consists of more than 1200 general and special rules. The general rules are related to synonyms, antonym and semantic roles etc., and special rules are about specific words. For instance, the general rule of synonyms is as follows.

```
~GeneralControl   0000 $@search (cd, SearchMode_First_Layer)!
```

In the above rule, "~ GeneralControl" is rule type which means this is a general rule, "$" is symbol of condition, "@" is symbol of conclusion, "cd" is current definition, and searching mode is "SearchMode_First_Layer". This rule is about searching definitions which contains specific definition fragment in the first layer. For example, given an input "airplane", relevant concept such as "passage" and "flight" would be found. The HowNet definition of "flight" is "DEF = {Number|编号:host = {aircraft|飞行器}}". For instance, special rule for "aircraft" to find "wreckage" is as follows.

```
aircraft|飞行器    0000
$c0[def={part|部件:RelateTo={mishap|劫难},modifier={incomplete|缺},
whole={vehicle|交通工具}}]@search(c0,SearchMode_Fuzzy)!
```

Tang [11] put forwards an unsupervised WSD method based on the sememe in HowNet. In this paper, we expand inference rules base on domain information, and use contexts of the polysemes as feature to improve the performance of disambiguation.

## 3    Automatic Construction Method of Knowledge Base

### 3.1    Headword Acquisition

Although most of domain terms themselves are not included in the knowledge base, but the headword such as "floodlight", "knob", "valve", "system", "assembly", "switch" and "sensor" are almost in HowNet knowledge base. According to the annotation rules of HowNet, value "1/2/3" of code in G_E is indicates that the record is a word, and "4/5/6" a phrase. Through the analysis of the knowledge base, it is found that the G_E and DEF of "AK-47步枪(AK-47 rifle)" and "步枪(rifle)" are as follows.

| AK-47 步枪 | G_E=noun [42riflenoun-0static 支   ] |
| | DEF={weapon|武器: domain={military|军},{firing|射击: instrument = {~}}} |
| 步枪 | G_E=noun [2 riflenoun-0static 支   ] |
| | DEF={weapon|武器: domain={military|军},{firing|射击: instrument = {~}}} |

The DEF of phrase "AK-47步枪(AK-47 rifle)" is consistent with the headword "步枪(rifle)", annotating terminology with definition of headword can resolve the scarce vocabulary and improve the efficiency of construction. Through the analysis, we found that headwords are usually at end of the compound words, therefore the headwords selected in the experiment are nouns at endings of the terms, as shown in Table 1.

### 3.2    Semantic Disambiguation of Headword

After headword acquisition, the DEF can be obtained. But some headwords have ambiguities such as "system" in Table 1 which corresponds to three DEFs. According to the statistics, for 125486 Chinese records in HowNet, there are 9.97% in which more than two concepts exist. It is therefore indispensable to do WSD for headwords

**Table 1.** Definition of terms headword in HowNet

| Headword | DEF of the headword | Terms |
|---|---|---|
| 泛光灯 (Flood Light) | {tool\|用具:{illuminate\|照射: instrument = {～}}} | "断路器板泛光灯","中央操 纵台泛光" etc. |
| 传感器 (Sensor) | {part\|部件:whole = {implement\|器具}, {sense\|感觉:instrument = {～}}} | "主起轮载传感器","转弯传 感器"etc. |
| 系统 (System) | {consistent\|有条理} | |
| | {part\|部件:PartPosition = {bone\|骨}, domain = {physiology\|生理学}, whole = {animate\|生物}} | |
| | {part\|部件:PartPosition = {bone\|骨}, whole = {artifact\|人工物}} | "姿态和航向基准系统","自 动调压系统","自动系统", etc. |

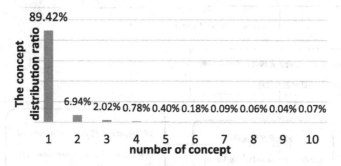

**Fig. 1.** Distribution of number of concepts

containing multiple DEFs. The distribution of number of concepts to which headwords correspond is shown in Fig. 1.

This paper adopts the disambiguation method of SCT in HowNet as baseline. For term of which headword has unique DEF doesn't do any WSD, but WSD would be done on the headword of term with multiple DEFs in the following process: (i) expanding the contextual features to the terms, (ii) do WSD with SCT base on expanded disambiguation rules, (iii) reorder the candidate list by target term and parts of speech. The specific workflow is shown in Fig. 2.

**Expansion of Contextual Features.** Terminologies are short texts, which are not abundant in semantic information, but by expanding the contextual features [12] such as bilingual sentences which contains terminologies to improve SCT performance by increasing the number of association between words. For example, the DEF selection process of the headword "阀(valve)" of the "液压系统优先阀(Hydraulic System Priority Valve)" is shown in Fig. 3.

It shows that without the context, the selected DEF of "阀" means "warlord", and the correct DEF is selected after the disambiguation with context as features. In this paper, before disambiguation, maximum length pairs of sentences in which the

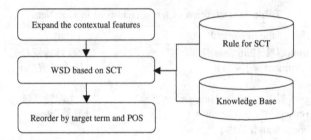

**Fig. 2.** Word sense disambiguation process for words with multiple definitions

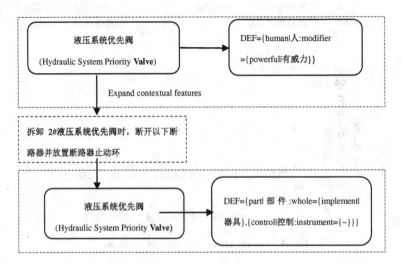

**Fig. 3.** DEF selection based on expanding contextual features

bilingual terms exist are selected as context, and then the disambiguation is carried out by taking the context as features.

**Disambiguation Based on SCT.** (*1*) *Expansion of WSD rules.* For the high-frequency words in corpus, this paper deals with disambiguation by expanding the rules. For example, "灯" appears for 211 times in the corpus with three different senses. The aircraft includes the flight equipment lights like "navigation lights", "cabin lights", "cargo door Lights", etc., and the existing disambiguation rules mostly contain common-sense knowledge association, and it is difficult to identify the association within the domain, such as "灯(light)" and "飞行器(aircraft)", therefore the association between knowledge is increased by adding rules for disambiguation.

```
~GeneralControl 0070
cd[def_son_class=={aircraft|飞行器}]$c0[def={illuminate|照射}] @search(c0,
SearchMode_Fuzzy)!
```

It is a general rule, and when the class of the DEF of the sub node of current DEF (cd) is "aircraft|飞行器", all the related records of lights about the aircraft can be searched by fuzzy searching (SearchMode_Fuzzy) fragment (c0) "DEF = illuminate|照射" to make association of the aircraft equipment with the lights, such as "L Wing Tip Position Light" and "NLG Fixed Taxi Light". The selection of the DEFs of the headword "灯" is shown in Table 2.

**Table 2.** Word sense disambiguation of headword "light"

| Before or after expand rules | Terminology | Headword | DEF = {tool\|用具: {WarmUp\|加热: instru-ment = {~}}, {burn\|焚烧: location = {~}}} | DEF = {tool\| 用具: {illuminate\| 照射: instrument ={~}}} | DEF = {part\|部件: Whole = {tool\| 用具}} |
|---|---|---|---|---|---|
| Before | 舱灯 | 灯(lamp) | | | √ |
| After | 舱灯 | 灯(lamp) | | √ | |
| Before | 左航行灯 | 灯(lamp) | | | √ |
| After | 左航行灯 | 灯(lamp) | | √ | |
| Before | 左翼根着陆灯 | 灯(lamp) | | | √ |
| After | 左翼根着陆灯 | 灯(lamp) | | √ | |

(2) *Optimization of WSD rules.* For another example, "器" appears for 287 times in the corpus with three different senses. For the term "作动器", the DEFs of "作", "动" and "器" are shown in Table 3.

**Table 3.** Definition of "作", "动" and "器"

| Word | DEF |
|---|---|
| 作(act) | {act\|行动} |
| 动(act) | {act\|行动} |
| 器 (utensil) | {Ability\|能力:host = {human\|人}} |
| | **{implement\|器具}** |
| | {part\|部件:domain = {physiology\|生理学},whole = {AnimalHuman\|动物}, {function\|活动:experiencer = {~}}} |

The Rule 1 is a special rule for DEF = {implement|器具} of "器", and any word of which first sememe is DEF = {act|行动} would be found. This rule will make sense to all the words before "器" with DEF = {act|行动}. Shield the Rule 1 and add the Rule 2 of common event class to "器" as follows.

```
Rule1 :    implement|器具   0000 $c0[def={act|行动}]@search(c0,SearchMode_First)!
Rule2:     ~Process_Event   0170 cd[def_class_h=={act|行动}]$c0[def={implement|器
具}] @search(c0,SearchMode_First)!
```

The "def_class_h" used in this rule is the Taxonomy (see Fig. 4), and if the hypernym of current DEF (cd) is the "act|行动" in the tree, all the words of which first sememe is "implement|器具" shall be found.

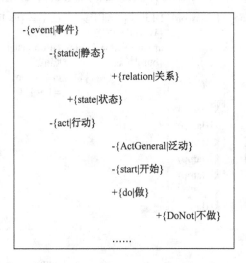

**Fig. 4.** Sememe Tree of event in HowNet Taxonomy

For Fig. 4 HowNet sememes taxonomy tree of event doesn't list all the sememes nodes, in which "+" indicates that this node contains nodes haven't been expanded and "–" indicates that this node has no other branch.

**Table 4.** Sample of word sense disambiguation rules

| Rule No. | Headword | Terminology |
|---|---|---|
| Rule 1 | 器 (utensil) | "供油切断阀作动器" and other terms end with "作动器". |
| Rule 2 | 器 (utensil) | "作动器" and other terms end with "作动器", "供油切断阀作动器", "蓄电池熔断器", "发电机接触器", "变阻器" etc. |

Both the Rule 1 and the Rule 2 can disambiguate the "器" in "作动器", and can do the same for other terms on top of that Table 4.

It can be found that Rule 2 of event class can disambiguate all the terms that the Rule 1 can, and for general rule is preferred than multiple special rules for common problems. Therefore, in the process of disambiguation of terms, the terms shall be first analyzed, the commonalities of the terms of the same types shall be summarized, and semantic disambiguation shall be carried out by means of the general rule instead of special rule. For example, the rule of entity class can be added to "器" in the previous example.

```
~Process_Entity    0200
cd[def_class_h=={inanimate|无生物}]$c0[def= {implement|器具}]@search(c0,
SearchMode_First)!
```

This rule disambiguates all the terms which entities are before "器", such as "积水器", "咖啡器", etc.

**DEF Reorder Based on Target Headword.** Through the expansion of the contextual features and disambiguation of SCT, the candidate list of the headwords of terms is obtained, and each candidate not only contains DEF information, but also the information of the translation and parts of speech to which the headwords correspond. Through the calculation of the similarity between the translations, the candidate reordering is carried out. For example, "MCDU MENU 键" obtains the first candidate DEF is "{part|部件: whole = {chemical|化学物}}" after SCT, but the optimal candidate DEF is "{part|部件: whole = {implement|器具}}" would be obtained by filtering "key" which is the translation of "键". The DEFs of "键" in the "MCDU MENU 键" are shown in Table 5.

**Table 5.** DEFs of headword "键"

| English Word | DEF |
| --- | --- |
| W_E = bond | DEF = {part|部件:whole = {chemical|化学物}} |
| W_E = key | DEF = {part|部件:whole = {implement|器具}} |
| W_E = bolt | DEF = {part|部件:whole = {implement|器具}, {fasten|拴连: instrument = { ~ }}, {fix|定住:instrument = { ~ }}} |

"MCDU MENU 键" corresponds to the English term "MCDU MENU Key" and the correct DEF option is selected according to the target headword.

### 3.3    Generation Algorithm of Term DEF

The annotations of DEF can be translated into headword DEF acquisition and disambiguation in the domain knowledge base construction. The terminology pair t whose concept is to be annotated is represented as 2-tuple t = <$t_{ch}$, $t_{en}$>, in which $t_{ch}$ represents the original of Chinese term, and $t_{en}$ represents the translation of English term. The bilingual sentence pair e = <$e_{ch}$, $e_{en}$> represented as the terminology pair appears; The sense s of HowNet is represented as s = <w_c, g_c, w_e, g_e, def>, in which w_c is the Chinese term, w_e is the English term, g_c is the part of speech of Chinese, g_c is the part of speech of English and def is the representation of concept.

---

**Generation algorithm based on the terms DEF headwords**

Input: Bilingual terminology **t**

Output: Field dictionary DEF **s**

Begin:

s = < $t_{ch}$, $t_{en}$, "", "", ""> // Initialization s

if $e_{ch}$ == "" then

   $e_{ch}$ = $t_{ch}$           // Get contextual information

endif

s.g_c = get_gc($t_{ch}$)      // Get phonetic information

seglist = segment($e_{ch}$)   // Get the word vector

list<list<unit>> ulist = disambiguation (seglist)

foreach nodelist in reverse_enumrate(ulist):

   foreach node in nodelist: // Reverse headword search

      if node is central word:

         s.def = node.def

         s.ge = get_ge(node)

      end if

   end for

end for

   return s
End

---

# 4   Experiment and Analysis

## 4.1   Corpus

This paper mainly performs automatic construction in the field of aviation, where bilingual terminology will be annotated. Aviation terminology has the following features.

Firstly, most terms are compound NPs. Statistics show that in the aviation corpus, 90.55% (21,136 /23,343) terms are compound NPs. We also counted 10,161 terminologies in patent, and the proportion is 90.84% (9230).

Secondly, there is large number of abbreviations in terminology. For instance, CB, ADV, PA, NWS, CDT are abbreviations which appear in the following terminologies.

| | |
|---|---|
| 断路器板泛光灯 | CB panel flood light |
| MENU ADV 旋钮 | MENU ADV Knob |
| 旅客广播接收旋钮 | PA Volume Control Knob |
| 球面框单向活门 | Bulkhead Check Valve |
| 空气总管系统 | Air Manifold System |
| 驾驶杆组件 | Control Column Assembly |
| 转弯解除开关 | NWS Disarming Switch |
| 压气机出口温度传感器 | CDT |

## 4.2  Experimental Results and Analysis

There are 3710 high-frequency and multi-concept words such as "device", "light", "system", "valve", "plate" in the corpus. 500 terms were randomly selected for testing and the rest of 3210 terms are used for analysis of headwords phenomenon, 8 rules were expanded for the HowNet SCT (not including the process of adding shielding filter rules). In the paper, we focus on aviation terminology construction. The maximum length of bilingual sentences is selected as contextual feature for term which correspond to more than two DEFs. Manual evaluation is made for the knowledge base construction experiment, and HowNet MT system based on the terminology knowledge is evaluated.

We performed statistics on the distribution of concepts corresponding to headwords in the 500 terms, as shown in Table 6.

**Table 6.** Concept distribution of term head-words

| Number of terms | Number of different headwords | Number of single concept headwords | Number of multiple concept headwords |
|---|---|---|---|
| 500 | 172 | 90 | 82 |

It can be seen that there're 82 (47.76%) headwords correspond to multiple concepts, which needs to be disambiguated. The WSD results are shown in Table 7.

**Table 7.** Manual evaluation result

| | Testing number | Correct number | Accuracy |
|---|---|---|---|
| Method of HowNet | 500 | 384 | 0.768 |
| Method in this paper | 500 | 431 | 0.862 |

Results shown that SCT of HowNet get 384 terms correctly annotated, which account for 76.8%. The method in this paper solve polysemous headwords by SCT where contexts are taken as features and rules are expanded, and got 431 correct terms

**Table 8.** Sample of annotation result

| Terminology | DEF after automatic construction |
|---|---|
| 外套螺母<br>(Sleeve Coupling **Nut**) | {part\|部件:whole = {implement\|器具}},{fasten\|拴连:<br>instrument = {∼}},{fix\|定住:instrument = {∼}}}} |
| 蓄电池控制器<br>(Battery **Controller**) | {part\|部件:whole = {implement\|器具}, {control\|控制:<br>instrument = {∼}}}} |
| 临近地板出口标志<br>(Lower Exit **Sign**) | {mark\|标志} |
| 液压系统优先阀<br>(Hydraulic System<br>Priority **Valve**) | {part\|部件:whole = {implement\|器具}, {control\|控制:<br>instrument = {∼}}}} |
| 外电源<br>(External Power) | {Source\|来源:host = {physical\|物质}} |
| 缘条<br>(Flange) | {part\|部件:PartPosition = {limb\|肢}, domain = {physiology\|生理<br>学}, whole = {plant\|植物}} |

accounting for 86.2% (increased by 9.4%). The results after construction are shown in Table 8.

The headwords "螺母" and "控制器" are single concept words, which don't need disambiguation. "标志", "灯" and "键" are multiple concepts, which need disambiguation. In the results, there are problems caused by the fault of word segmentation, such as "外电源" segmented as "外电 源" for which there is something wrong with annotations. "缘条" as a complete word in HowNet are segmented as "缘" and "条".

### 4.3 Results Analysis of Machine Translation

HowNet MT is a rule-based and semantic-based system by the knowledge base. We evaluate the translation results from two aspects, namely the accuracy and fluency of the target text. Specific criteria are shown in Tables 9 and 10.

**Table 9.** The evaluation criteria of accuracy

| Score | Express degree of the original text |
|---|---|
| 5 | all the original meaning |
| 4 | most of the original meaning |
| 3 | more original meaning |
| 2 | Communicate less original meaning |
| 1 | Did not express the original meaning |

Knowledge base construction is carried out for the annotated terms by means of HowNet browser, the experiment of HowNet MT System are made before and after construction. 50 sentences which contain terminologies in 500 terms are randomly selected. The test was scored by 5 professional translators before and after the results of the construction, and the evaluation was made according to Tables 9 and 10. The evaluation results are shown in Table 11.

**Table 10.** The evaluation criteria of fluency

| Score | Express degree of the original text |
|-------|-------------------------------------|
| 5 | Fluent Chinese |
| 4 | Better Chinese |
| 3 | Non-native language |
| 2 | Non-fluent Chinese |
| 1 | Expression is not clear in Chinese |

**Table 11.** MT manual evaluation result

| | Accuracy | Fluency |
|---|----------|---------|
| Before construction | 2.78 | 2.88 |
| After construction | 3.01 | 2.98 |

Result shows that the construction of the knowledge base can significantly improve the Rule-based MT system. Not only the expansion of bilingual term, but also the syntactic and semantic information improves the performance of HowNet MT system. For example, terms containing verb may destroy the structure of sentences during semantic analysis before expanding knowledge base and the problem was alleviated by the terminology knowledge.

# 5 Conclusion

This paper realizes automatic construction of domain terminology knowledge base based on the headword of a terminology. Headword disambiguation is done by considering the context of headwords and adding domain-specific disambiguation rules to the general disambiguation rules. Experiments on aviation domain show that our proposed method on headword disambiguation achieves 9.4% improvement over the default disambiguation tools in HowNet. We also find that with our automatically constructed domain terminology knowledge bases, HowNet machine translation system achieves better translation quality.

For HowNet MT System, not only domain knowledge bases and the scenario-based disambiguation rules are required, but also the expansion of the translation rules. And The RBMT has a certain advantage in the framework translation and long-distance reordering, and the SMT has an advantage in word selection. Following work will expand the HowNet translation rules and complete the fusion of RBMT and SMT.

# References

1. Dong, Z., Dong, Q.: HowNet. http://www.keenage.com
2. Wang, Y., Bai, Yu., Ding, C.: Construction of TCM theoretical knowledge base for semantic retrieval. J. Chin. Inf. Process. **26**(5), 72–78 (2012)

3. Zhang, G., Diao, L., Diao, P.: Construction of aviation termiology semantic knowledge base based on HowNet. J. Chin. Inf. Process. **28**(5), 92–101 (2014)
4. Liu, J., Tang, H., Tang, H.: Semantic knowledge base constructed from chinese online encyclopedia. J. Syst. Simul. **28**(3), 542–548 (2016)
5. Cui, L., Chen, Q.C., Guo, H.Z., Wang, X.L.: Auto-extraction approach of sematic class attributes in the fusion of HowNet and Wikipedia. In: Advances of Computational Linguistics in China (2009)
6. Dong, Z., Dong, Q., Hao, C.: Semantic computing in HowNet MT system. In: CWMT 2014, pp. 45–54 (2014)
7. Dong, Z., Dong, Q.: HowNet and the Computation of Meaning. World Scientific, Singapore (2006)
8. Dong, Z., Dong, Q.: HowNet and its computation of meaning. In: International Conference on Computational Linguistics: Demonstrations, vol. 88(8), pp. 301–306 (2010)
9. Dong, Z., Dong, Q., Hao, C.: Theoretical findings of HowNet. J. Chin. Inf. Process. **21**(4), 3–9 (2007)
10. Dong, Z., Dong, Q., Hao, C.: Sense colony testing in HowNet MT system. In: CWMT 2014, pp. 55–63 (2014)
11. Tang, G., Yu, D., Xun, E.: An unsupervised word sense disambiguation method based on the representation of sememe in HowNet. J. Chin. Inf. Process. 06 (2015)
12. Yang, Z.: Word sense disambiguation method based on knowledge context. J. Comput. Appl. **35**(4), 1006–1008 (2015)

# Building the Vietnamese Phrase Treebank by Improved Probabilistic Context-Free Grammars

Ying Li[1,2], Jianyi Guo[1,2(✉)], Zhengtao Yu[1,2], Yantuan Xian[1,2],
and Yonghua Wen[1,2]

[1] The School of Information Engineering and Automation, Kunming University
of Science and Technology, Country Kunming, Yunnan 650500, China
gjade86@hotmail.com
[2] The Key Laboratory of Intelligent Information Processing,
Kunming University of Science and Technology,
Country Kunming, Yunnan 650500, China

**Abstract.** Phrase Treebank is an important resource for Natural Language
Processing research and practical application. For Vietnamese, we lack this kind
of Treebank resources. This paper presents a method to construct the Vietnamese phrase Treebank by fusion of Vietnamese grammatical features and
improved PCFG. This method can automatically analyze Vietnamese phrase
structure tree and solve the problem of constructing the Vietnamese phrase
Treebank. Firstly, Vietnamese grammatical feature set is established by analysis
of Vietnamese grammatical features. Then, grammar rule set of PCFG model is
obtained from manual annotation Vietnamese phrase trees. Finally, Vietnamese
grammatical feature set is fused into improved PCFG model, which is regarded
as a supplement, and the method completes the construction of Vietnamese
phrase Treebank. The experimental results show that the accuracy of proposed
PCFG model for the Vietnamese phrase Treebank construction reaches 89.12%.
Compared to conventional PCFG model and the maximum entropy method, the
accuracy obviously is improved.

**Keywords:** Vietnamese · Phrase structure tree · Probabilistic context-free
grammar · Grammatical rule set · Treebank introduction

## 1 Introduction

The construction of Phrase Treebank plays a very important role in the study of linguistics, such as syntactic pattern extraction and the survey of linguistic phenomena. At
the same time, it is often used to training tools for word segmentation, Syntactic analysis
and semantic role labeling. These tools are the basis of information extraction, machine
translation, question and answer system and text classification applications [1]. In recent
years, with the rapid development of machine learning and artificial intelligence,
automatic construction of phrase Treebank become more and more important [2].

Phrase syntactic analysis is that automatic sliding derive sentence grammatical
structure according to a given grammar system. It also can analyze contain grammatical

© Springer Nature Singapore Pte Ltd. 2016
M. Yang and S. Liu (Eds.): CWMT 2016, CCIS 668, pp. 75–90, 2016.
DOI: 10.1007/978-981-10-3635-4_7

unit and the relationship between grammatical unit (Allen 1995) [3]. Finally, it transforms a sentence to structured syntactic tree. The phrase tree consists of three kinds of symbols, which are in accordance with the specific grammatical rules. Some terminal nodes constitute a phrase. At the same time, it plays as a non-terminal character involved in a reduction until the whole sentence reduce for root node [4].

Syntactic analysis and construction of phrase Treebank have the function of mutual promotion. The phrase Treebank provides the objective text annotation data for the theoretical study [5]. Syntactic analysis has always been the focus of Natural Language Processing's research, but also a major obstacle to Natural Language Processing research progress. Syntactic analysis can be simply divided into two types, which are the early method that is based on rule and the statistical method [6]. The statistical method becomes current mainstream method. The rule mainly relies on linguists to write rules to describe the syntax of language, which is based on linguistic theory [7]. Through this set of grammar rules, the syntax structure can be deduced when you put in a text string. Linguists believe that the structure of all human languages is a hierarchical structure. The hierarchical structure can be expressed in the form of rules, and the set of rules is the syntax [8]. Rule-based method is a very tedious process. In addition, the cost of development rules is very large, and it is difficult to find an effective way to improve the efficiency of rule development. With the construction of the corpus, more and more attention has been paid to statistics syntax analysis, which has become the mainstream method in the field of Natural Language Processing [9]. This method uses statistical processing techniques to acquire the knowledge of language analysis from large scale corpus, and it tries to approach the true rule of language. Statistical parsing is required to complete two tasks. The first task is to establish a language model for the resolution of syntactic ambiguity. The second task is to find the Maximum probability value of all the syntax trees. Then, the Maximum probability tree is output from the model.

At present, the most successful Treebank is the Penn Treebank for English, which greatly promotes the syntactic analysis of English, and it has become the standard of English syntactic analysis (ET, Al, Marcus, [10], 1993). Success of Penn Treebank increased researcher's attention to the construction of the Treebank. The construction of other languages Treebank has also been launched. For example, the University of Pennsylvania developed for English phrase structure Treebank PET (about 300,000 words) in 1994; the University of Pennsylvania built for Chinese phrase structure Treebank PCT (about 25 million words) in 2003 [11]; Tsinghua University constructed the Chinese phrase structure Treebank TCT973 in 2003 (about one million words) [12]; Saarland University developed for German phrase structure Treebank tiger in 2002 (about 3.5 million words) [13].

There is little study of the Vietnamese phrase Treebank. The studies of Vietnamese mainly include three aspects. Nguyen C T, Nguyen T K (2006) completed the Vietnamese word segmentation work which is based on CRF and SVM model [14]. Le H Nguyen (2006) proposed lexical chain grammar, but he didn't illustrate how to use the grammar to construct phrase tree [15]. Nguyen PT et al. (2009) introduced the research about construction of Vietnam syntax tree, but they didn't give detailed experimental results. Dinh Dien et al. (2009) built English - Vietnamese parallel bilingual syntactic tree for Machine Translation. Vietnamese syntax tree constructed in this paper has many problems. For instance, English and Vietnamese can't correspond one to one. It will lead to accuracy rate of Vietnamese syntactic tree is very low [17].

Due to the lack of Vietnamese phrase Treebank, this paper proposes a fusion Vietnamese grammatical features and improved PCFG method to construct Vietnamese phrase Treebank. The method can automatically analyze Vietnamese phrase structure tree, and it solves the problem of constructing the Vietnamese phrase Treebank. Firstly, the inside-outside algorithm gets model PCFG grammar rule sets from the manual annotation of Vietnamese phrase tree. Secondly, Vietnamese language feature set is established by analysis of Vietnamese grammatical features. Finally, the grammatical feature set as well as grammatical rule set into a PCFG model, and the new model complete construction of Vietnamese phrase Treebank.

## 2  Formulation of Vietnamese Language Feature Set

Vietnamese belongs to South Asian languages, and it is the national language of Vietnam. Every language has its own order. Vietnamese mainly relies on the composition to convey important grammatical information. Vietnamese has three obvious characteristics, which is different from the western language. Some Vietnamese characteristics have the extremely important influence on Vietnamese phrase Treebank construction:

(1) The smallest unit of Vietnamese is syllable. Words can only be made up of one (đẹp | beautiful) or more (cô gái | girl) syllables. Vietnamese hasn't text delimiter like many Asian Languages (such as Chinese, Japanese and Thai). Space is a syllable separator, and it hasn't a division of word, So Vietnamese sentences can often have many kinds of segmentation methods.

(2) Vietnamese is an isolated language. Word doesn't change its form but according to word order to determine its grammatical function in this language. That is to say that word order is the most important means of Vietnamese grammar meaning in the table. Word order change will result in semantic change. For instance, "người còn" is son while "còn ngườ" is human. Word order of Vietnamese sentence is gradually enhanced. The more general meaning of the word, the more previous position it gets in the sentence. On the contrary, the more specific meaning of the word, the more back position it gets in the sentence. For example, "Anh đã mua" | he bought "một quả táo" | an apple.

(3) Vietnamese is a relatively fixed word order language, and a fixed word order is SVO (SVO). That is to say, they generally order: subject + predicate + object. For example, "Kia" | that "là" | is "những" | some "nhà"| house. Through the analysis of Vietnamese grammatical features, it can be found that there are some obvious characteristics of Vietnamese such as Post-attributes and Post-Adverbials. For instance, "Tôi thường ăn" | I often eat "ở quán ăn tự phục vụ"| in the canteen.

According to the characteristics of Vietnamese, this paper adopts the artificial method of making Vietnamese language feature set. The Vietnamese language feature set will be used for the construction of Vietnamese phrase tree, which is fused in the PCFG model as a supplement of the probability of grammar rules. Part of the Vietnamese language feature set is shown in Table 1. In given Table 1, the main part of

Table 1. Part set example of Vietnamese language features

| Grammatical rules | Probability value |
|---|---|
| PP -> E NP | 0.5 |
| PP -> E | 0.5 |
| ADJP -> R A | 0.4 |
| ADJP -> A R | 0.1 |
| ADJP -> R A C | 0.3 |
| ADJP -> A | 0.2 |

Table 2. Vietnamese Treebank constituency tags

| Constituency tag | Description |
|---|---|
| NP | Noun phrase |
| PP | Prepositional phrase |
| VP | Verb phrase |
| ADJP | Adjective phrase |
| AP | Adverb phrase |
| QP | Quantitative phrase |

Vietnamese language characteristics formulated is according to the characteristics of Post-attributes and Post-Adverbials. Part of the constituency tags are shown in Table 2.

## 3  Improved PCFG Method

### 3.1  Introduction of PCGF Probability Model

Probabilistic context free grammar is a grammar rule system which is introduced into the context free grammar rule system [18]. At present, the research of context free grammar is mainly to improve the accuracy of the independent hypothesis. This paper also introduces the syntactic analysis model of the concept of syntactic structure, to improve the accuracy of PCFG model analysis.

The input sentence is $S = w_1 w_2 \ldots w_n$ ($w_1^n$). Then, using statistical methods gets the maximum syntactic tree $\varphi$, which eventually achieved max $P(\varphi/S)$. The parser returns a syntax tree $T(S)$.

$$T(S) = \text{argmax}_\varphi P(\varphi, S)/P(S) = \text{argmax}_\varphi P(\varphi, S) \tag{1}$$

Firstly, probability values of all possible parse tree are calculated. Then, the maximum values of $P(\varphi/S)$ is selected. Finally, it is regarded as the result of final analysis.

PCFG is a probabilistic extension of context free grammar. It assigns a probability value to each production rule, which extends the description system of context free grammar (CFG) [19]. With PCFG, the probability value of the syntax tree can be obtained by calculating the probability of all the production rules used in the tree, which is $P(\varphi, S)$. The equation of the form such as:

$$P(\varphi, S) = \prod_{r \in \varphi} P(r) \tag{2}$$

Formula (2) is based on the three independent assumptions of PCFG: context independent, location independent, and ancestor independent.

However, natural language has a strong contextual relevance. Combined with Vietnamese characteristics described previously, this paper adds some parts of speech and the syntactic co-occurrence information. It is regarded as a new method to measure the probability values of syntax tree. Two definitions are introduced. One is forward co-occurrence probability, and another is backward co-occurrence probability.

Definition of 1: the forward co-occurrence probability $Q$ $(V, C)$ of syntactic analysis refers to the probability that word v appears in front of syntactic category C. It meets the limit:

$$\forall v \sum_{C \in V_n} Q(v, C) = 1 \tag{3}$$

Definition of 2: syntactic analysis of the backward co-occurrence probability $H$ $(V, C)$ refers to the probability that word v appears behind syntactic category C. It meets the limits:

$$\forall v \sum_{C \in Vn} H(v, C) = 1 \tag{4}$$

Two co-occurrence probabilities are added to the formula for calculating the probability of the syntax tree. The Vietnamese language feature probabilities, the sub-tree probabilities, as well as co-occurrence probabilities are jointly to determine the probability of syntactic tree.

We assume that the probability of leaf node is 1. The following is the calculation method of probability for non leaf nodes. Hypothesis $A_{mn}$ expresses $A \Rightarrow w_m \ldots w_n$, which are the phrases $w_m \ldots w_n$. The phrases are derived by sub-tree. Then the assumption of non-terminal expansion rules is r: $A \rightarrow X_1 X_2 \ldots X_k$. The probability of sub-tree is jointly determined by the probability of a rule R, the probability of each $X_i$, forward co-occurrence probability and backward co-occurrence probability. So we use the arithmetic mean of these probabilities as the probability value of sub-tree $A_{mn}$. The formula is shown as (5):

$$P(A) = \frac{P(r) + \sum_{i=1}^{k} P(X_i) + Q(v_{m-1}, A) + H(v_{n+1}, A)}{k+3} \tag{5}$$

Compared with the traditional PCFG model, the formula (5) can get a more equitable evaluation result of the syntax tree. So it can get a more reliable and optimal syntax tree.

## 3.2  Acquisition of Grammatical Rules

The probability value of grammar rules is generally achieved by the method: first of all, the rules and the number of rules are added up in the training corpus; then, the probability value of rules is estimated from frequency of rules appearing by using the maximum likelihood estimation; finally, the probability is a rule value [20]. The calculation formula is

$$P_r(A \rightarrow X) = \frac{C(A \rightarrow X)}{\sum_{\gamma \in (V_T \cup V_N)} C(A \rightarrow Y)} \tag{6}$$

$C(A \rightarrow X)$ represents the number of rule $A \rightarrow X$, which appears in the Treebank. $P_r(A \rightarrow X)$ is the probability value of rule $A \rightarrow X$.

The method mentioned above has a large dependence on the training corpus. The scale and quality of the corpus are directly related to the accuracy of the probability values of the grammatical rules. But Vietnamese Treebank's scale is relatively small in the current. This method cannot reflect the real Vietnamese language rules.

The method used in this paper is that the initial probability of generating rules is changed. Firstly, Inside-Outside algorithm is used to calculate the initial set of rules in the Treebank; then, EM algorithm is used to train the training corpus, which can get a convergent PCFG grammar. In order to minimize the dependence of training corpus, the formula (6) is used to obtain the initial estimate of the rule. The procedure is as follows:

Firstly, a threshold of Y is set. Rule set will be divided into high frequency rule set (HFR) and low frequency rule set (LFR). Rules are

$$HFR = \{A \rightarrow X | P_r(A \rightarrow X) > \gamma\} \tag{7}$$

$$LFR = \{A \rightarrow X | P_r(A \rightarrow X) \leq \gamma\} \tag{8}$$

Secondly, we assume that M is the number of rules in the LFR set, and N is the sum of all the rules in the HFR.

$$N = \sum_{(A \rightarrow X) \in HFR} P_r(A \rightarrow X) \tag{9}$$

Thirdly, the formula (10) and (11) are used to obtain the initial probability values for the initial iteration.

$$P_r(A \rightarrow X) = \alpha \times \frac{P_r(A \rightarrow X)}{N} \text{ if } A \rightarrow X \in HFR \tag{10}$$

$$P_r(A \rightarrow X) = \frac{(1 - \alpha)}{M} \text{ if } A \rightarrow X \in LFR \tag{11}$$

The $\alpha$ range is 0–1, which is the sum of the estimated probability values of all the rules in the HFR set. At the same time, $(1 - \alpha)$ is the sum of the probability values of the rules in the LFR set. In this paper, the $\alpha$ value is 0.91.

### 3.3    The Calculation Method of Co-occurrence Probability

The method of Vietnamese co-occurrence probability calculation is maximum likelihood estimation in this paper. The calculation formula is

$$Q(\varepsilon, C) = \frac{\text{Count(C is at the beginning of the sentence)}}{\text{Count(All syntactic category appears in front of sentence)}} \tag{12}$$

$$Q(v, C) = \frac{\text{Count(V appears in front of C)}}{\text{Count}(v)} \tag{13}$$

A similar method for calculating backward co-occurrence probability is

$$H(\varepsilon, C) = \frac{\text{Count(C is at the end of the sentence)}}{\text{Count(All syntactic category appears at the end of sentence)}} \tag{14}$$

$$H(v, C) = \frac{\text{Count(V appears at the end of C)}}{\text{Count}(v)} \tag{15}$$

In this paper, a simple smoothing method is used to solve the data sparse problem. For the above formula (12) to (15) can use a unified formula (16) to express:

$$P = \frac{M}{N} \tag{16}$$

P is the requirement's probability. M is a molecule, which is a statistical frequency. N is the denominator, which is a total. When the statistics of M is zero, i/N can be expressed 1/N. the probability of other conditions is calculated according to the formula (17):

$$P = \frac{M}{N}\left(1 - \frac{i}{N}\right) \text{(i is the number of 0 probability events)} \tag{17}$$

## 4    The Construction of the Treebank Vietnamese Phrase

Probabilistic model of Vietnamese syntactic analysis provides computational syntax tree probability method. And it also provides a method to find the most possible phrase tree when some syntactic ambiguities exist. The syntactic parsing algorithm is used to realize the probability model of syntactic analysis. The syntactic parsing algorithm used in this paper is an extension of the GLR algorithm. It is based on the GLR algorithm, and it fused the Vietnamese language feature set and Vietnamese grammar probability set in GLR algorithm.

Traditional GLR parsing algorithm: the first step, a sentence syntactic analysis of the forest is obtained, and that is the acquisition of all possible phrase tree; the second step, the probability of each tree possible phrase tree is calculated; the third step, the maximum probability of the phrase structure tree is picked out as a result of the final analysis. In this paper, the traditional GLR parsing algorithm is improved, which can be used in the acquisition of syntax analysis of the forest at the same time to pick out the highest probability of the phrase tree as the final analysis of the results.

In this paper, firstly, production is preprocessed. All the FIRST collection and FOLLOW collection of terminator and non-terminator are obtained according to the production set. Automata grammars are constructed, which are based on the first set, follow collection and production set. Finally, GLR parsing table is generated, which is based on the self motivation.

# 5    Experimental Results and Analysis

## 5.1    The Experimental Data

Experimental data in this paper mainly includes two parts: one corpus is used to acquire the rules of grammar phrase tree, which are 10000 manual annotation Vietnamese phrase trees. 9000 sentences are regarded as training corpus, and 1000 sentences are regarded as a test corpus. Using the training corpus statistics Vietnamese grammar rules and calculates initial probability value. Another is 18,000 Vietnamese sentences, which are used to construct the Vietnamese phrase tree. The Vietnamese sentences are mainly from China Radio International Vietnamese section navigation. The navigation bar includes the press, radio, blogs, forums, learning Chinese and entertainment thirteen modules. Crawling web pages forms a text corpus through rules extraction, weight, machine tagging, manual calibration steps. The scale of text corpus is 25981 Vietnamese sentences, and the encoding of method uses UTF-8. Finally, the Vietnamese sentences are processed with Vietnamese POS tagging platform SVMTool for Vietnamese word segmentation and part of speech tagging. These sentences access to high quality of the test corpus after manual correction. The Test corpus of Vietnamese phrase Treebank is shown in Table 3.

**Table 3.** Test corpus of Vietnamese phrase Treebank

| Category of Corpus | Number of files | Number of sentences | Average length of sentences |
|---|---|---|---|
| news | 121 | 3000 | 21.30 |
| radio | 92 | 2000 | 20.69 |
| forum | 115 | 2500 | 23.54 |
| blog | 53 | 1000 | 17.32 |
| academia | 120 | 3000 | 19.14 |
| wiki | 140 | 4000 | 18.56 |
| entertainment | 109 | 2500 | 19.07 |
| total | 750 | 18,000 | 21.27 |

## 5.2 Evaluation Method

We use PARSEVAL syntax analysis and evaluation system, which is an international standard evaluation criteria. It includes three indicators, which are the precision (LP), the recall (LR) and the F-score. F-score is comprehensive consideration of the accuracy and recall rate. Its definition is as follows [20]:

$$\text{precision} = \frac{\# \text{ of correct constituent in hypothesis}}{\# \text{ of total constituents in hypothesis}} \qquad (18)$$

$$\text{recall} = \frac{\# \text{ of correct constituent in hypothesis}}{\# \text{ of correct constituents in reference}} \qquad (19)$$

$$F = \frac{2 * \text{precision} * \text{recall}}{\text{precision} + \text{recall}} \qquad (20)$$

## 5.3 Analysis of Experimental Results

1. The selection of test subset

Test corpus is divided into 18 test subset, which will be used to construct Vietnamese phrase Treebank. Each test set contains 1000 Vietnamese sentences, which are treated with word segmentation and part of speech tagging tools. 8 test subsets are extracted from 18 test subset. In order to ensure the diversity of the test data, 200 sentences are achieved from in different corpus categories. The first 4 test subsets are regarded as closed test sets, and the remaining 4 groups are regarded as open test sets. Details of the selected 8 test subsets are shown in Table 4.

**Table 4.** Data of test subsets

| Test subsets | The number of sentences | Average length of sentence |
| --- | --- | --- |
| Test subset 1 | 1000 | 19.82 |
| Test subset 2 | 1000 | 23.65 |
| Test subset 3 | 1000 | 18.51 |
| Test subset 4 | 1000 | 17.37 |
| Test subset 5 | 1000 | 20.39 |
| Test subset 6 | 1000 | 22.95 |
| Test subset 7 | 1000 | 19.07 |
| Test subset 8 | 1000 | 18.30 |

2. Using the improved PCFG method to construct Vietnamese phrase Treebank

Vietnamese Treebank is constructed by PCFG method which fuses the Vietnamese grammatical features. Firstly, analysis of the Vietnamese language features make Vietnamese language feature set. Then, the initial grammar probability set is obtained from 9000 manual annotation Vietnamese phrase tree by the inside outside algorithm.

Finally, the Vietnamese language feature set is regarded as the supplement of Vietnamese initial grammar probability set. Vietnamese phrase structure tree is constructed by improved PCFG method. Experimental result of 8 test subsets is shown in Table 5, and Fig. 1 gives a more intuitive results. The comparison of exprimental results on open and closed test subset is shown in (Figs. 2, 3 and 4).

**Table 5.** Experimental results based on the method proposed in this paper

| Test subset | 1 | 2 | 3 | 4 | 5 | 6 | 7 | 8 | Average |
|---|---|---|---|---|---|---|---|---|---|
| LP% | 83.12 | 79.51 | 82.52 | 83.31 | 77.57 | 78.37 | 76.23 | 78.38 | 79.88 |
| LR% | 82.57 | 78.86 | 81.69 | 82.03 | 76.62 | 77.35 | 75.81 | 77.23 | 79.02 |
| F-value% | 82.84 | 79.18 | 82.1 | 82.67 | 77.09 | 77.86 | 76.51 | 77.8 | 79.51 |

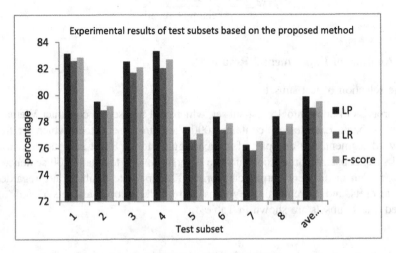

**Fig. 1.** Experimental results of test subsets based on the proposed method

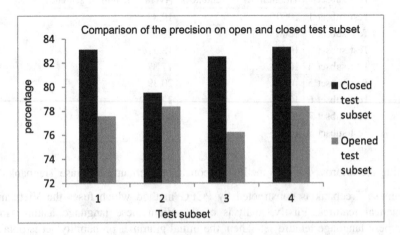

**Fig. 2.** Comparison of the precision on open and closed test subset

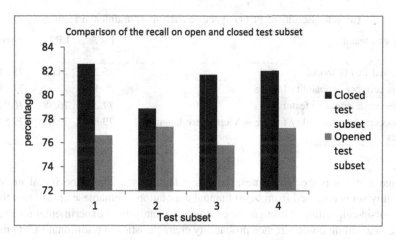

**Fig. 3.** Comparison of the recall on open and closed test subset

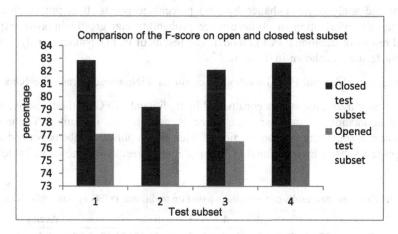

**Fig. 4.** Comparison of the F-score on open and closed test subset

It can be found that the results of open test sets are obviously worse than results of closed test sets. This was due to Vietnamese grammar rules can not cover all Vietnamese sentences which are used in this paper. At the same time, because the grammar rule set is extracted from the existing manual annotation Treebank, it cannot cover all the grammar rules in the open test environment.

3. Using the improved PCFG method with diffrent features to construct Vietnamese phrase Treebank

In order to accurately assess accuracy of Vietnamese phrase tree construction which is used the proposed improvement PCFG model, this paper respectively joins the Vietnamese language features and co-occurrence probability characteristics to do contrast test. The test results are shown in Table 6. Firstly, analysis of the Vietnamese

**Table 6.** Results of PCFG syntactic analysis with different features

| Model and feature | LR% | LP% | F-score % |
|---|---|---|---|
| Traditional PCFG model | 76.26 | 74.43 | 75.31 |
| + Co-occurrence probability feature | 78.15 | 77.02 | 77.58 |
| + Vietnamese language features | 77.24 | 76.58 | 76.91 |
| + Co-occurrence probability feature + Vietnamese language features | 79.88 | 79.02 | 79.51 |

language features make Vietnamese language feature set. Then, the initial grammar probability set is obtained from 9000 manual annotation Vietnamese phrase tree by the inside outside algorithm. Through the comparative analysis of experimental results, we can see that adding co-occurrence probability characteristics in traditional PCFG model brings F-value promote by 2.27 percentage points. In addition, when co-occurrence feature and characteristics of Vietnamese language are added to the model, the results of syntactic analysis can enhance by 1.93 percentage points. It is proved that the characteristic information of co-occurrence probability can greatly improve experimental results of traditional PCFG model. The results of PCFG syntactic analysis with different features is shown in Table 6.

## 4. Using the traditional PCFG method to construct Vietnamese phrase Treebank

Vietnamese phrase Treebank is constructed by traditional PCFG method. Firstly, 5000 manual annotation Vietnamese phrase tree is used to get the initial Vietnamese grammar rule set. Then, the construction of Vietnamese phrase Treebank is conducted on eight test subsets by traditional PCFG model. Test results are shown in Table 7.

**Table 7.** Experimental results of test subsets based on traditional PCFG syntax analysis method

| Test subset | 1 | 2 | 3 | 4 | 5 | 6 | 7 | 8 | Average |
|---|---|---|---|---|---|---|---|---|---|
| LR% | 78.12 | 77.39 | 78.35 | 78.96 | 74.25 | 75.37 | 73.28 | 74.34 | 76.26 |
| LP% | 76.57 | 75.62 | 76.46 | 76.59 | 72.12 | 73.85 | 71.32 | 72.89 | 74.43 |
| F-score % | 77.34 | 76.49 | 77.39 | 77.56 | 73.17 | 74.60 | 72.29 | 73.61 | 75.31 |

## 5. Using the maximum entropy method to construct the Vietnamese phrase Treebank

Vietnamese phrase Treebank is constructed by maximum entropy method. First of all, 5000 manual annotation Vietnamese phrase tree is regarded as the training corpus to construct maximum entropy model. Then, Vietnamese phrase Treebank is constructed by the maximum entropy model with the above extraction of eight test subsets. The experimental results are shown in Table 8.

In this paper, Vietnamese phrase Treebank is constructed by traditional PCFG model, maximum entropy model and improved PCFG model which fuses Vietnamese language characteristics and co-occurrence probability feature. At the same time, the

**Table 8.** Experimental results of test subsets based on maximum entropy analysis method

| Test subset | 1 | 2 | 3 | 4 | 5 | 6 | 7 | 8 | Average |
|---|---|---|---|---|---|---|---|---|---|
| LR% | 80.86 | 79.37 | 80.01 | 81.28 | 76.30 | 77.52 | 76.08 | 76.94 | 78.55 |
| LP% | 78.31 | 77.28 | 78.45 | 79.60 | 74.12 | 75.85 | 74.39 | 74.87 | 76.61 |
| F-score % | 79.56 | 78.31 | 79.22 | 80.43 | 75.19 | 76.68 | 75.23 | 75.89 | 77.56 |

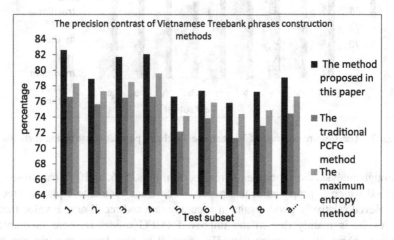

**Fig. 5.** The precision contrast of Vietnamese Treebank phrases construction methods

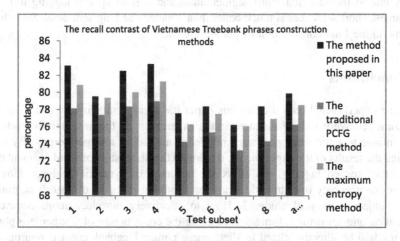

**Fig. 6.** The recall contrast of Vietnamese Treebank phrases construction methods

accuracy rate, recall rate, F-value of Vietnamese phrase Treebank are analyzed and calculated. Thus, validating the improved PCFG method is most suitable for the Vietnamese phrase Treebank construction method. Comparison experimental results are shown in Figs. 5, 6, and 7.

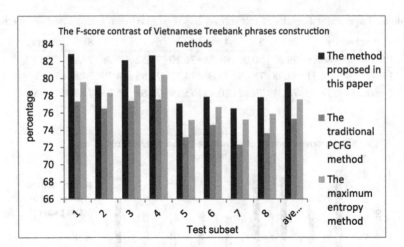

**Fig. 7.** The F-score contrast of Vietnamese Treebank phrases construction methods

Through analysis the experimental results from Figs. 5, 6, and 7, It can be seen that the method which is proposed in this paper to construct Vietnamese phrase Treebank have achieved relatively good results in accuracy rate and recall rate, F value method. These results is mainly due to the improved PCFG model is more favorable for Vietnamese phrase tree construction. However, it is also found that the results of Vietnamese short sentences are much better than Vietnamese long sentences. This is mainly due to the fact that word segmentation and part of speech tagging tools for Vietnamese short sentences is much better than Vietnamese long sentences. So it direct impacts on the final construction of phrase Treebank.

# 6   Conclusions

Since the experimental date used in this paper has some limitations, it can only deal with some relatively simple sentences in the experiment. In the next step of work, we will continue to enrich the grammar knowledge and adopt a larger corpus. By summarizing the results of the experiments, it is found that the results of word segmentation and part of speech tagging will affect the accuracy of syntactic analysis. How to improve the accuracy of automatic word segmentation and part of speech tagging is also a subject worthy of study. 2. How to effectively introduce more contextual information and semantic information to guide the construction of Vietnamese phrase Treebank will be directly related to Vietnamese phrase Treebank construction quality. It is important one of our future works.

**Acknowledgment.** This work was supported in part by the National Natural Science Foundation of China (Grant Nos. 61262041, 61363044 and 61472168) and the key project of National Natural Science Foundation of Yunnan province (Grant No. 2013FA030).

# References

1. Johnson, M.: PCFG models of linguistic tree representations. Comput. Linguist. **24**(4), 613–632 (1998)
2. Hajic, J.: Building a syntactically annotated corpus: the prague dependency Treebank. Issues of Valency and Meaning, pp. 106–132 (1998)
3. Le, H.P., Nguyen T.M.H., Romary, L., et al.: A lexicalized tree-adjoining grammar for vietnamese. Lrec. (2006)
4. Nguyen, C.T., Nguyen, T.K., Phan, X.H., et al.: Vietnamese word segmentation with CRFs and SVMs: an investigation. International Conference on languages, Information and Computing in the Asia Pacific Region (2006)
5. Dien, D., Ngan, T., Quang, X., et al.: The parallel corpus approach to building the syntactic tree transfer set in the english-to-vietnamese machine translation. Quím. Nova **32**(6), 1477–1481 (2009)
6. Le-Hong, P., Nguyen, T.M.H., Azim, R.: Vietnamese parsing with an automatically extracted tree-adjoining grammar. In: Proceedings of the IEEE International Conference in Computer Science: Research, Innovation and Vision of the Future, RIVF, HCMC, Vietnam (2012)
7. Nguyen, P.T., Xuan, L.V., Nguyen, T.M.H., Le Hong, P.: Building a large syntactically annotated corpus of Vietnamese. In: Proceeding of the 3th Linguistic Annotation Workshop, ACL-IJCNLP, Singapore, pp. 182–185 (2009)
8. Le Hong, P., Ho, T.V.: A maximum entropy approach to sentence boundary detection of Vietnamese texts. In: Proceedings of IEEE International Conference on Research, Innovation and Vision for the Future – RIVF 2008, Vietnam (2008)
9. Cherry, C., Lin, D.: A comparison of syntactically motivated word alignment spaces. EACL (2006)
10. Dukes, K., Habash, N.: One-step statistical parsing of hybrid dependency-constituency syntactic representations. In: International Conference on Parsing Technologies. Iwpt 2011, 5–7 October 2011, Dublin City University, Dubin, Ireland, pp. 92–103 (2011)
11. Hong, P.L., Nguyen, T.M.H., Roussanaly, A.: Vietnamese parsing with an automatically extracted tree-adjoining grammar. In: IEEE Rivf International Conference on Computing and Communication Technologies, Research, Innovation, and Vision for the Future, pp. 1–6 (2012)
12. Ting, L., Shan, M.J.: Theory and method of Chinese automatic syntactic parsing. Contemp. Linguist. **2**, 100–112 (2009)
13. Li, J., Mu, L., Zan, H., Zhang, K.: Research on chinese parsing based on the improved compositional vector grammar. In: Lu, Q., Gao, H. (eds.) Chinese Lexical Semantics. LNCS (LNAI), vol. 9332, pp. 649–658. Springer, Heidelberg (2015). doi:10.1007/978-3-319-27194-1_64
14. Huang, Z., Harper, M.: Self-training PCFG grammars with latent annotations across languages. In: EMNLP, pp. 832–841 (2009)
15. Ule, T.: Directed Treebank refinement for PCFG parsing. The Workshop on Treebanks & Linguistic Theories, pp. 523–530 (2003)
16. Zhang, K., Zan, H., Han, Y., et al.: Preliminary study on the construction of bilingual phrase structure Treebank. Lect. Notes Comput. Sci. **8922**, 403–413 (2014)
17. Carroll, B.G., Rooth, M.: Valence induction with a head-lexicalised PCFG. In: Conference on Empirical Methods in Natural Language Processing (2013)

18. Hong, P.L., Nguyen, T.M.H., Roussanaly, A.: Vietnamese parsing with an automatically extracted tree-adjoining grammar. In: IEEE Rivf International Conference on Computing and Communication Technologies, Research, Innovation, and Vision for the Future, pp. 1–6 (2012)
19. Langlais, P., Gotti, F.: Phrase-based SMT with shallow Tree-Phrases. In: The Workshop on Statistical Machine Translation. Association for Computational Linguistics, pp. 39–46 (2006)
20. Carpenter, B.: The generative power of categorial grammars and head-driven phrase structure grammars with lexical rules. Comput. Linguist. **17**, 301–314 (1999)

# Classifying Commas for Patent Machine Translation

Hongzheng Li[(⊠)] and Yun Zhu

Institute of Chinese Information Processing, Beijing Normal University,
Beijing, China
lihongzheng@mail.bnu.edu.cn, zhuyun@bnu.edu.cn

**Abstract.** Commas are widely distributed and used in Chinese and play important role in detecting boundary of basic units in sentences and discourses. Towards Chinese-English patent machine translation, this paper presents two methods using rich linguistic information to identify commas which separate sub-sentences and non-sub-sentences. The first method employs word knowledge base and formal rules to determine roles of commas, while the second one uses machine learning approaches. The experimental results show that overall F1 scores of rule-based method are higher than 93%, indicating the approach performs well in classifying commas. On the other hand, the classifiers show some differences. We also draw the conclusion that identifying commas is actually able to improve the quality of translation outputs.

**Keywords:** Comma · Rule · Machine learning · Patent machine translation

## 1 Introduction

As one of the most important punctuations, commas are widely used in Chinese patent texts, having several functions in the sentences. In which two basic functions are end of sub-sentence (EOS) and end of words or phrases, i.e. None EOS (NEOS). In the paper, the sub-sentence are defined as dependent components of a whole sentence, they are top-level children in the syntax trees, and there must be a predicate verb in the sub-sentence.

Different with newswire or other domain texts, sentences in patent texts are usually much longer, with more characters, and the syntactic structures tend to much more complex, furthermore, they often involve amounts of specific terminology in various fields, such as chemistry and biology. A long patent sentence ($S$) ended with a full stop can be composed of several sub-sentences ($SS$), connected by commas or some other punctuations such as semicolons, in which the SS can further contain kinds of phrases and chunks.

Here is an example sentence from patent text and its syntax tree:

[SS1在上述结构中, 单电池由突起部支撑], [SS2因此可以提高耐振动性。] (In above structures, the single cell is supported by the protrusions, therefore the vibration resistance can be improved.)

The example includes two sub-sentences connected by an EOS comma, and there is a NEOS comma in the first sub-sentence. (Fig. 1)

© Springer Nature Singapore Pte Ltd. 2016
M. Yang and S. Liu (Eds.): CWMT 2016, CCIS 668, pp. 91–101, 2016.
DOI: 10.1007/978-981-10-3635-4_8

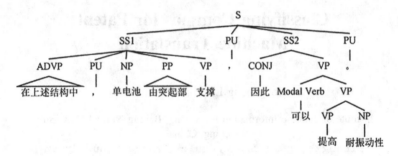

**Fig. 1.** Syntax tree of the example sentence

Correct disambiguation and classification of commas is a necessary step to detect sentence boundaries, which will further have positive impacts on many tasks and applications in Natural Language Processing (NLP) such as parsing and Machine Translation (MT). In this paper, towards Chinese-English patent MT, we present two methods with rich linguistic information to identify the EOS and NEOS commas. The first method is featured with knowledge base and formal rules which describe the linguistic and contextual information. The method is conducted within a parser which is integrated in a Chinese-English patent MT system (Li et al. 2015) to parse the sentences and identify the commas. In the second approach, we train three machine learning classifiers (Maximum Entropy, Naïve Bayes and Decision Tree) to classify the functions of commas.

We then carry out experiments to testify the performance of the proposed approaches, overall F1-measure of rule method are higher than 93%, indicating its effectiveness and feasibility. But when comparing results of the two approaches, the differences are remarkable. Translation evaluation tests also prove that identifying commas is beneficial to improve the quality of translation outputs.

The rest of this paper is organized as follows: Sect. 2 discusses some related works, Sect. 3 describes commas in Chinese patent texts briefly, Sect. 4 presents the rule-based identification method in detail, Sect. 5 proposes the machine learning approach, Sect. 6 conducts experiments and gives some analysis, and the last section concludes the work.

## 2  Related Works

In recent years, Chinese comma has gradually attracted amounts of research from the viewpoint of natural language processing, including sentence segmentation, discourse analysis and other perspectives.

Jin (Jin et al. 2004) and Li (Li et al. 2005) proposed that Chinese comma disambiguation is part of "divide-and-conquer" strategy to syntactic parsing. Long sentences are split into shorter sentence segments on commas before they are parsed, and the syntactic parses for the shorter sentence segments are then assembled into the syntactic parse for the original sentence.

Xue and Yang (2011) viewed Chinese comma disambiguation as the detection of loosely coordinated clauses separated by commas, which are syntactically and semantically complete on their own and do not have a close syntactic relation with one another. They (Yang and Xue 2012) further pointed out that the Chinese comma signifies the boundary of discourse units and also anchors discourse relations between adjacent text spans, and they proposed a discourse structure oriented classification of the comma that can be automatically extracted from the Chinese Treebank (CTB) based on syntactic patterns. Similar works are also conducted later, using some machine learning approaches to disambiguate and classify the Chinese commas (Xu and Li 2013; Li 2013; Li 2014; Gu et al. 2015).

Kong and Zhou (2013) employed a comma disambiguation method to improve syntactic parsing and help determine clauses in Chinese. In order to address the problem that performance of Chinese comma disambiguation usually heavily depends on the performance of syntactic parser, they then proposed a joint approach combining k-best parse trees to reduce the dependent on parsing (Kong and Zhou 2014).

Many previous works are based on newswire texts, mainly based on the CTB corpus, and use machine learning methods such as CRF, Maximum Entropy and Decision Tree. Besides the news corpus, some works also study commas in patent domain texts from the aspect of patent machine translation (Zhu et al. 2012; Li et al. 2015). In this paper, we will also conduct research on identifying and classifying commas in Chinese patent documents.

## 3   Commas in Chinese Patent Texts

As mentioned, most sentences in patent texts are much longer and may contain more than one comma, and positions of these commas are quite flexible, they can follow words (W), phrases (P) or sub-sentences (SS). As a result, theoretically, commas can separate 9 different types of elements in the sentence. Let's take the following patent sentence example to state the combinations.

[P在本发明的一个方面], ①[P被沉积的墨水], ②[W例如], ③[W喷墨], ④[SS可以被进行处理], ⑤[P在另一方面], ⑥[SS把它们进行固化], ⑦[SS然后通过紧缩方式形成本发明的防伪特征], ⑧[W例如], ⑨[P样本中的反射性防伪特征]。 (In an aspect of the present invention, the deposited ink, e.g., ink jet, may be treated, in another aspect, they are cured, and form the security features of the invention by compression, e.g., reflective security feature in the sample.) (Table 1)

Table 1.  Type of elements connected by each comma

| Combination | Position of comma |
| --- | --- |
| SS+SS | ⑦ |
| SS+W | ⑧ |
| SS+P | ⑤ |
| W+W | ③ |
| W+P | ⑨ |
| W+SS | ④ |
| P+W | ② |
| P+P | ① |
| P+SS | ⑥ |

Clearly, only commas in the first three combinations can be recognized as EOS, as they follow the SS, and the remaining are all NEOS commas.

After analyzing the sentences in patent corpus, we've found that the "SS+SS" type accounts for the highest proportion, almost about 50% of total sentences, followed by the type "P+SS", in which phrases most are noun phrases (NPs), prepositional phrases (PPs) and adverbial phrases (ADVPs). Such distribution once again the importance of commas and its identification.

Note that, commas in some specific terms or formulas of chemical field (for example, "5-oxo-4, 5-dihydro-1, 2, 4-oxadiazol-3-yl") should not be identified as EOS or NEOS comma. And they will be preprocessed in advance before the identification, Sect. 4 will discuss this in detail.

# 4   Rule-Based Methods

There exists many fixed structures and expressions from word-level to sentence-level in patent texts, such fixed structures are more suitable to be described by formal rules. That's why we decide to use rule-based method to identify and classify the commas. In this part, we will discuss the approach with some rules and example sentences.

## 4.1   Identification Procedures

Figure 2 shows the processing steps in identifying the commas, we will describe each stage in the following.

**Preprocessing.** In patent sentences, there are amounts of supplementary statements that appear in brackets, they usually have negative impacts on analyzing the regular structures. Thus we need to delete them to guarantee the parsing as much as possible (as shown in Table 2). On the other hand, special terms and expressions containing commas, which are not related to detection of the boundaries of sentences and chunks, also need to be deleted. Note that, preprocessing should guarantee the meaning and syntactic structures of sentences are not affected.

Next, **word segmentation** are conducted based on conditional random field (CRF) approach (Lafferty et al. 2001). Then the sentences will be separated into strings by commas, semicolons and colons in the step of **sentence segmentation**.

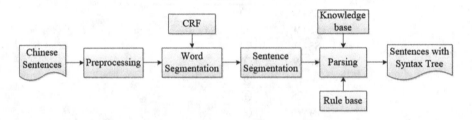

**Fig. 2.** Rule-based identification procedures

**Table 2.** An example of preprocessing

| Before preprocessing | After preprocessing |
|---|---|
| 在一些实施例中，可以使用其他数目的虚拟天线/信道(例如，一个或更多个)。 | 在一些实施例中，可以使用其他数目的虚拟天线/信道。 |
| In some embodiments other numbers of virtual antennas/channels (e.g., one or more) may be used. | In some embodiments other numbers of virtual antennas/channels may be used. |

Finally, in **parsing** process, the parser will generate a syntax tree for each sentence, and the commas will be classified and tagged with corresponding symbols on the tree.

Knowledge base and rules are necessary for rule-based methods in NLP. For the identification of commas, we have built a Chinese word knowledge base consisting more than 30,000 words which are all extracted from the Chinese patent corpus provided by the *State Intellectual Property Office of China (SIPO)*[1]. The words are annotated with various syntactic and semantic information. Note that, besides words, some common fixed expressions like parenthesis, "也就是说*(that is to say)*", for example, are also included. We also manually wrote formal identification rules in the form of Backus-Naur Form (BNF) based on linguistic analysis of various contextual information in the sentences.

## 4.2 NEOS Identification

In patent texts, it is common that a whole sentence often begins with monosyllables (such as "即" (that is)), conjunctions(marked as "LB"), parenthesis, as well as fixed expressions, followed by commas. These elements can usually recognize such commas as NEOS commas (marked as "DBT").

On the other hand, kinds of NPs, PPs and ADVPs at the beginning of a sentence can also be separated from other chunks by NEOS commas. In these phrases, there are many collocations between the left and right boundary words. As for NPs serving as subject, a fixed typical NP is that begins with the word "一种*(a/an)*" as modifier and ends with head NP such as "方法*(method)*/装置*(device)*/系统*(system)*". As for PPs, types and structures have been discussed in (Li et al. 2014), and collocation expressions between left and right boundary words like "当……时 *(when……)*" "在……中 *(in)*" are widely used.

All these features and linguistic information are beneficial to determine the commas as NEOS. In the rules, we need to pay more attention to exploit such important information.

Here are some rules and examples.

(−1){LC_CHK[LB]&BEGIN%} + (0)CHN[,] =>LC_TREE(DBT,0,0)
(−1){LC_CHK[NP, PP, ADVP]&BEGIN%} + (0)CHN[,] =>LC_TREE(DBT,0,0)
(b){(−1)LC_CHN[一种]&BEGIN%} + (0)CHN[,] =>LC_TREE(DBT,0,0)

---

[1] http://www.sipo.gov.cn/.

The Arabic numbers in the rules indicate positions of nodes in the string, and the left parts of the rule indicate the contextual information of the commas while the right parts show that they will be marked with the DBT node on the syntax tree.

e.g. [S [Conj.而且], [PP在该实施例中], [NP一种用于预防或治疗哺乳动物中循环系统疾病的方法], [SS其可以包括任何一项的化合物。]] (Furthermore, in this embodiment, a method for preventing or treating of circulatory diseases in a mammal can include any one of the compounds.)

### 4.3　EOS Identification

As for identification of EOS comma (marked as "SST" on the syntactic tree), the conjunctions is a useful clue once again. But different with those in NEOS, the conjunctions here usually introduce sub-sentences at the beginning. These conjunctions can either appear as collocations in a pair, such as "虽然……,但是……*(although……)*" "不但……,而且……*(not only……,but also……)*", or singly used, for example, "同时 *(meanwhile)*" "以便*(so that)*", to express various discourse semantic relationships. Once commas appear together with such conjunctions, there is usually high possibility that the comma is EOS.

We try to find out all the possible conjunctions representing semantic relationships exhaustively to cover the contexts that commas may appear, and put them into the rules.

Here we give some rules which represent causal, conditional and progressive relationship respectively.

(b){(−1)LC_CHK[LB]&CHN[因为,因,是因为,为的是,由于]} + (0)CHN[,] + (1) LC_CHK[LB,LA]&CHN[所以,因此,因而,故,就,便,才,之所以] =>LC_TREE (SST,0,0)

(b){(−1)LC_CHK[LB]&CHN[如果,假如]} + (0)CHN[,] + (f){(1)LC_CHK[LB] &CHN[将,则,那么]} =>LC_TREE(SST,0,0)

(0)CHN[,] + (1)LC_CHK[LB]&CHN[继而,进而,直到,直至] =>LC_TREE (SST,0,0)

But, a question is, not all sub-sentences are introduced by conjunctions and have explicit discourse relationship, under such situation, then how to identify the commas? We suppose the key problem is to identify the core verb first.

Since sub-sentences are defined as sentences which must contain predicate verb, only the predicate is recognized, can we know that the strings before the comma are really sub-sentences instead of phrases or chunks, then can we make sure that the comma is EOS. That means, identifying such EOS actually depends on the recognition of core verbs.

To solve the problem, we utilize a weight-ranking strategy (Zhu et al. 2012; Li et al. 2015) to identify corn verb from several verbs in the same sentence. The basic idea is, series of weights representing the possibilities to be predicate are designed, after excluding some verbs that definitely cannot be core verb, remaining possible verbs will obtain corresponding weights based on contextual, syntactic and semantic information after matching kinds of rules. The verbs with the highest weight will be selected as predicate verb finally. Once the predicate verb are recognized, the comma will be EOS and tagged with SST consequently.

Sum up, in the process of identify EOS and NEOS commas, the rules always try to capture and use linguistic and contextual information which are helpful and effective to the identification. In most cases, the left and right boundary words of phrases or sub-sentences are especially useful for chunking and parsing.

## 5 Machine Learning Classification

Disambiguating the two roles of commas can be considered as the binary classification problem. In this part, we will train the Maximum Entropy (ME), Naïve Bayes (NB) and Decision Tree (DT) classifiers with the Mallet[2] machine learning package to classify the Chinese commas.

Considering the specific characteristics of patent texts, we adopt some of features used in (Xue and Yang 2012) and (Li et al. 2013), and also design some new features for the classifiers based on linguistic analysis of patent corpus. The final features can be divided into three types: lexical, phrasal and syntactic features.

Taking the simple example "在上述结构中，单电池由突起部支撑。" for instance, we will describe the features as follow. (Table 3)

**Table 3.** Features for training the classifiers

| Features | Statement of features | Examples |
|---|---|---|
| Lexical features | The Combination of first and last words and part of speech (POS) in the strings before the commas. | F1 = 在 + 中, F2 = P+LC |
| | The first word and its POS behind the comma, and whether the POS is conjunction. | F3 = 单电池, F4 = NN, F5 = No |
| | Whether the string before the comma is just a single word. | F6 = No |
| | Whether the string before the comma contains core predicate and conjunctions. | F7 = No, F8 = No |
| Phrasal features | Whether the string before the comma is NP. | F9 = No |
| | Whether the string before the comma is ADVP. | F10 = No |
| | Whether the string before the comma is PP. | F11 = Yes |
| Syntactic features | The phrase label of the left sibling and right sibling of the comma on the syntactic tree, as well as their conjunction. | F12 = PP, F13 = IP, F14 = PP + IP |
| | The conjunction of the phrase label of the left sibling, the parent node and the phrase label of the right sibling. | F15 = PP + S+IP |
| | Whether the comma is a top-level child in the syntactic tree. | F16 = Yes |

---

[2] http://mallet.cs.umass.edu/.

# 6  Experiments and Analysis

In this part, we will conduct experiments to testify the performance of the two proposed methods, using precision rate (P), recall rate (R) and F1-measuere as measure metrics.

In order to find out whether identifying commas has influence on the quality of translation, we also use BLEU evaluation to compare the performance of MT system without adding comma identification rules and system with these rules.

## 6.1  Data Setting

We take the development set of Chinese-English patent MT test on NTCIR-9[3] as test set, which contains 2000 bilingual patent sentence pairs. Sentences without commas were excluded, and the final test set contains 1666 sentences with 3110 commas, in which 1747 were EOS, occupying about 56.17%, and the remaining 1363 (43.83%) were NEOS commas.

In the rule-based test, we will use the parser to parse the sentences and analyze commas on each syntactic tree to determine the performance.

In the machine learning test, after labelling the test set with features, we divide the total set into training data set and testing data set with the proportion of 80%: 20%, and employ 10-times, 10-fold cross-validation policy to test the classification performance.

## 6.2  Results

Tables 4 and 5 show the final classification results of the two methods. And Table 6 shows BLEU evaluation of two systems.

## 6.3  Analysis

**Rule-base method.** As can be seen from Table 4, F1 scores of the two kinds of commas are all over 93%, the precision rates even higher than 95%. The figures have clearly proved that our approach performs well in disambiguating roles of commas, and it is effective and feasible. Performance of EOS is a little better than NEOS.

**Table 4.** Rule-based classification results of commas

|      | Total | Identified | Correct | P (%) | R (%) | F1 (%) |
|------|-------|-----------|---------|-------|-------|--------|
| EOS  | 1747  | 1780      | 1706    | 95.84 | 97.65 | 96.74  |
| NEOS | 1363  | 1262      | 1231    | 97.54 | 90.45 | 93.86  |

---

[3] http://research.nii.ac.jp/ntcir/permission/ntcir-9/perm-en-PatentMT.html.

More specifically, for EOS, recall rate was higher than precision rate by about 2%, however, the situation was just opposite for NEOS, in which recall rate was 7% lower than precision rate. While recall rate of NEOS was also lower than that of EOS, the precision rate of NEOS was a litter higher than that of EOS.

After analyzing the test results, we've found some following reasons accounting for improper or error identification.

To begin with, word segmentation error could lead to incorrect results. For example, in the NP "在/蜂窝/网络/上/传递/的/辅助/信息,"(the assistance information delivered over the cellular network), the italic string "上传递" was mistakenly segmented as "上传/递", and "上传*(upload)*" was identified as predicate verb, the NP was parsed as a sentence, as a result, the NEOS comma was mistakenly considered as EOS.

Second, some words, such as "在(ZAI)/为(WEI)", are multi-category word which can be verb or preposition in different sentences. Error analysis of such words may also has negative impacts on commas. For example, in the sub-sentence "这种应用程序可以在SIM卡内,……" (The application can be in the SIM card,……), the word "在" tended to be a verb, but the system parsed it as preposition and the sentence as ADVP, thus the SST comma was marked as DBT.

Last, phrases with ambiguous structures could lead to erroneous identification. Especially for those NP modified by only verb instead of other adjectives or numerals. Such NPs were more likely to be parsed as VP or sentences.

For example, "另一个沉积墨水的方法的例子,例如,可喷射墨水或数字墨水,可以减少墨水组分的粘度。" (Another example of a method for depositing the ink, e.g., an sprayable ink or digital ink, can decrease the viscosity of the ink composition.)

According to the context, the italic part was actually a NP, and "可喷射*(sprayable)*" was the modifier of "墨水(ink)". However, it was parsed as VP (i.e. spray the ink), in which "ink" become object of "喷射", and the word "可" was recognized as modal verb "can". Thus the NP was identified as a sub-sentence at last. Correspondingly, the NEOS comma behind NP was incorrectly classified as EOS.

**Machine Learning Approach.** Regarding the results of machine learning tests in Table 5, we will also give some analysis. First of all, the overall results indicate that the Naïve Bayes classifier overweighed other two. This is different with conclusion in Li's work (Li et al. 2013), in which it indicated that ME classifier was the best one based on CTB6.0 corpus.

In our experiments, similar to rule-based results, the precision rates of NEOS were still much higher than recall rates, we suppose the main reason lies in that, the structures and expressions of non-sentence units such as NPs and PPs are more fixed in

**Table 5.** Machine learning classification results of commas

|  | EOS | | | NEOS | | |
|---|---|---|---|---|---|---|
|  | P (%) | R (%) | F1 (%) | P (%) | R (%) | F1 (%) |
| DT | 74.27 | 98.75 | 84.64 | 94.25 | 40.01 | 55.24 |
| ME | 74.82 | 98.24 | 84.53 | 94.37 | 40.67 | 55.23 |
| NB | 74.56 | 99.16 | **84.96** | 96.32 | 40.03 | **55.64** |

**Table 6.** Comparison of MT systems

| System | BLEU |
|---|---|
| Without comma rules | 11.28 |
| With comma rules | 11.44 |

patent texts, and they possess more obvious features, thus they are more easily and correctly identified with no matter rule-based or classification approaches.

Comparing the results of the two approaches, we can also find out some similarities. For example, precision rates were all lower than recall rates in EOS, but situation was opposite in NEOS. And F1 scores of NEOS were all lower than those of EOS. But it is quite surprising that, in the rule-based test, F1 of NEOS was only about 3% lower than that of EOS, but the differences even become 30% in the machine learning tests! One possible reason for the result may be the number of NEOS examples was less than EOS in the test set.

**BLEU Comparison.** Finally, from Table 6, after adding identification rules related to commas to the MT system, its performance is better than the system without the rules, and the BLEU score increased from 11.28 to 11.44. It clearly indicates that identifying commas correctly does have positive impacts on improving the quality of final translation outputs.

## 7   Conclusion

In this paper, based on rich linguistic information, we proposed two methods to identify commas, which serve as sub-sentence boundaries and non-sub-sentence boundaries in Chinese patent texts. The first one is a rule-based method, in which we built a knowledge base and wrote formal linguistic rules to disambiguate the commas. The second is training classifiers with machine learning toolkit. We then conducted experiments to testify the performance of the proposed approaches. Experimental results have proved that the rule-based approach performs well in the identification, although there also existed some error results. And the Naïve Bayes classifier performed best in the machine learning test. On the other hand, there is big differences between the results of the two approaches, which is much worth further researching.

In the future, we will pay more attention to address the reasons resulting in error identification, we will also explore more useful features and expand the test set, trying to improve further performance.

## References

Jingjing, G., Zhou, G.: Chinese comma classification based on segmentation and part of speech tagging. Comput. Eng. Appl. **51**(18), 120–125 (2015). (In Chinese)

Jin, M., Kim, M.-Y., Kim, D., Lee, J.-H.: Segmentation of chinese long sentences using commas. In: Proceedings of the SIGHANN Workshop on Chinese Language Processing, pp. 1–8 (2004)

Kong, F., Zhou, G.: A clause-level hybrid approach to Chinese empty element recovery. In: Proceedings of the Twenty-Third International Joint Conference on Artificial Intelligence, pp. 2113–2119 (2013)

Kong, F., Zhou, G.: Chinese comma disambiguation on k-best parse trees. In: Zong, C., Nie, J.-Y., Zhao, D., Feng, Y. (eds.) Proceedings of CCF Conference on Natural Language Processing & Chinese Computing. CCIS, vol. 496, pp. 13–22. Springer, Heidelberg (2014)

Lafferty, J., McCallum, A., Pereira, F.: Conditional random fields: probabilistic models for segmenting and labeling sequence data. In: Proceedings of 2001 International Conference on Machine Learning, pp. 282–289 (2001)

Li, H., Zhao, K., Hu, R., Zhu, Y., Jin, Y.: A hybrid system for chinese-english patent machine translation. In: Proceedings of 6th Workshop on Patent and Scientific Literature Translation of MT Summit 2015, pp. 52–67 (2015)

Li, H., Zhu, Y., Yang, Y., Jin, Y.: Reordering adverbial chunks in Chinese-english patent machine translation. In: Proceedings of 3rd IEEE International Conference on Cloud Computing and Intelligence Systems, pp. 375–379 (2014)

Li, X., Yang, H., Huang, J.P.: Maximum entropy for Chinese comma classification with rich linguistic features. In: Proceedings of the Third CIPS-SIGHAN Joint Conference on Chinese Language Processing, pp. 11–17 (2014)

Li, X., Zong, C., Hu, R.: A hierarchical parsing approach with punctuation processing for long sentence sentences. In: Proceedings of the Second International Joint Conference on Natural Language Processing, pp. 17–24 (2005)

Li, Y., Feng, W., Zhou, G., Zhu, K.: Research of Chinese clause identification based on comma. Acta Scientiarum Naturalium Universitatis Pekinensis 49(01), 7–14 (2013). (In Chinese)

Prasad, R., Dinesh, N., Lee, A., Miltsakaki, E., Robaldo, L., Joshi, A., Webber, B.: The penn discourse TreeBank 2.0. In: Proceedings of the 6th International Conference on Language Resources and Evaluation, LREC 2008 (2008)

Xu, S., Li, P.: Recognizing Chinese elementary discourse unit on comma. In: Proceedings of 2013 International Conference on Asian Language Processing, pp. 3–6 (2013)

Xue, N., Yang, Y.: Chinese sentence segmentation as comma classification. In: Proceedings of the 49th Annual Meeting of the Association for Computational Linguistics, pp. 631–635 (2011)

Yang, Y., Xue, N.: Chinese comma disambiguation for discourse analysis. In: Proceedings of the 50th Annual Meeting of the Association for Computational Linguistics, pp. 786–794 (2012)

Zhu, Y., Jin, Y.: A method of recognizing the root of an improved dependency tree for the Chinese patent literature. In: Proceedings of IEEE CCIS 2012, p. 1 (2012)

# BLEUS-syn: Cilin-Based Smoothed BLEU

Junting Yu[1], Wuying Liu[2(✉)], Hongye He[1], and Mianzhu Yi[1]

[1] Luoyang University of Foreign Languages, Luoyang, China
junting_yu@163.com, hugh5945@163.com,
13373781261@163.com
[2] Laboratory of Language Engineering and Computing,
Guangdong University of Foreign Studies, Guangzhou, China
wyliu@gdufs.edu.cn

**Abstract.** Machine Translation (MT) evaluation is very important for a MT system. In this paper, we investigate an improved Cilin-based smoothed BLEU (BLEUS-syn). As the possible cases that the short translation or English abbreviations in candidate may cause unigram have no matches, this evaluation metric smoothed the traditional BLEUS n-gram. It applied synonym substitution in unigram matching, and calculated the other 2–4-gram. It performed experiments in Russian and Chinese bilingual sentence data set and evaluated the output translations of online translation systems such as Google, Baidu, Bing and Youdao. The experimental results show that the effectiveness of our BLEUS-syn and traditional BLEUS are consistent. The performance of Baidu is the best, that of Youdao is the second, and that of Bing is the worst. Using BLEUS-syn can greatly enhance the performance of traditional BLEUS evaluation. It makes the Baidu BLEUS value improve 6.81%, Youdao improve 6.98%, Google 7.82%, and Bing 7.55%.

**Keywords:** Cilin · Evaluation · BLEU · BLEUS

## 1 Introduction

With the popularity of Internet and the arrival of the era of big data, Internet languages become more and the contacts of various countries become more frequent. As the main platform of information, the language translation becomes the key factor. With the multi-language information processing, traditional human translation cannot meet the daily needs, and the machine translation, which can translate multi-language automatically, become a hot topic. With the continuous development of information technology, translation quality, various machine translation systems and models appear. The translation quality and performance index become critical for the machine translation system. The evaluation of MT systems becomes important for the research of machine translation.

Machine translation evaluation usually refers to the quantitative evaluation of a given translation system. It can evaluate the system performance and enable the developers to learn the problems and improve it in time. The text evaluation of MT system mainly has two kinds of human evaluation and automatic evaluation, which is provided in the language specification released by the State Language Work Committee [1]. The human evaluation is mainly scoring the adequacy and fluency of system output by language

© Springer Nature Singapore Pte Ltd. 2016
M. Yang and S. Liu (Eds.): CWMT 2016, CCIS 668, pp. 102–112, 2016.
DOI: 10.1007/978-981-10-3635-4_9

experts subjectively according to references. But the human translation has many shortcomings, such as strong subjectivity, expensive, easy to be affected by external factors, the long evaluation period and so on. These will cause the human translation unable to adapt to the progress of MT system modification and parameter optimization, extend the system development period, and difficult to provide developers and users with efficient evaluation. As a result, researchers prefer the automatic evaluation.

Automatic evaluation methods can be divided into three categories: the linguistic point of detection, string similarity and machine learning. The linguistic point of detection method proposed by Professor Y Shiwen [2], is not widely used because it doesn't consider the whole of translation and tests the corresponding part of the translation according to the prior definition of a good linguistic test points, which cost higher. The method based on the string similarity becomes the most widely used evaluation method among the single metric evaluation. The best one is BLEU, which is proposed by Papineni [3] in 2002. BLEU matches the n-gram between candidate and reference, and the more n-gram match, the higher score is. Then researchers have made a lot of improvements against the problems such as not applied to sentence level and lack of recall. The most famous and widely used are the smoothed BLEU (BLEUS) [4], ROUGE-N [5] and METEOR [6]. The machine learning method develops fast as the emergence of deep neural networks and the multi-features evaluation.

In view of the maturity of the application, the operating speed and the degree of application, in this paper, we propose a new metric BLEUS-syn based on Cilin [7] and smoothed BLEU [8]. We adopt the synonym match except the exact word match in BLEU smoothing technology to improve the evaluation metric performance.

## 2    BLEUS-syn Metric

### 2.1    Smoothing BLEU

Papineni [3] has proposed the first evaluation metric BLEU based on n-gram in 2002. Then it is widely used in various evaluations. BLEU is calculated through matching the n-grams between candidate and reference. We take the geometric mean of the test sentences' modified precision scores and then multiply the result by a brevity penalty factor (BP). BLEU is defined as:

$$\text{BLUE} = \text{BP} \times \exp\left(\sum\nolimits_{n=1}^{N} w_n \log p_n\right) \tag{1}$$

And the N is the maximum base element of n-gram, $p_n$ is the precision of n-gram, $w_n$ is the weight of n-gram. Generally, the N is set 4 and $w_n$ is $1/N$. The brevity penalty BP is defined as Formula (2), which is used to compensate the lack of recall.

$$\text{BP} = e^{\min(1-r/c,0)} \tag{2}$$

However, the original BLEU is designed for the corpus-level. When any n-gram precision is zero, the final geometric mean will be zero. So BLEU is short of meaningful sentence-level score, which is important for distinguishing system performance.

In order to compute BLEU at sentence level, we apply smoothing technique to deal with the zero precision.

Lin [4] has proposed smoothing BLEU for the first time. Add one count to the n-gram hit and total n-gram count for n > 1, which is shown as Formula (3). Therefore, for candidates with less than n words, we can still get a positive smoothed BLEU score from shorter n-gram matches. If nothing matches BLEU will be zero.

$$p_n = \frac{Count_{clip(n-gram)+1}}{Count_{(n-gram)+1}} \tag{3}$$

$Count_{clip(n-gram)}$ is the minimum n-gram number in candidate translation, and $Count_{(n-gram)}$ is that in reference translation. And the BLEUS is calculated as Formula (4).

$$BLEUS = \min\left(e^{(1-r/c)}, 1\right) \times \exp \sum_{n=1}^{N} w_n \log p_n \tag{4}$$

## 2.2  Word Similarity Computation Based on Cilin

Diversification of language expression increases the difficulty of information processing. Different systems will produce different translations for the same source language. Semantic analysis and synonym match are important for MT evaluation. Word similarity is the base of research on metric evaluation, and it is important for improving metric performance.

The semantic dictionary, such as WordNet, HowNet and Cilin, leads the word similarity computation to be a hot spot.

### 2.2.1  Cilin Introduction

Cilin is a semantic dictionary compiled by Mei Jiaju and other scholars and published in 1980s. Then Information Retrieval Laboratory in Harbin Institute of Technology completes HIT IR-Lab Tongyici Cilin (Extended) through deleting not widely used words and dictionary expansion, which contains 77,343 words finally [7].

Cilin contains not only synonym words, but relevant words. Only the leaf nodes of its tree hierarchy are sets of words. Concept is the smallest unit of semantic description, and the tree hierarchy is shown as Fig. 1.

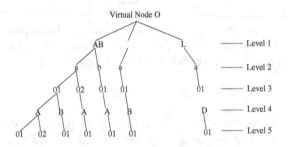

**Fig. 1.** Cilin tree hierarchy

Five level coding is used in Cilin. The uppercase letters of the alphabet are adopted to represent the major category; medium category with a lowercase letter; minor category is represented by two decimal integers; the fourth level is called word group adopting uppercase letters of alphabet; the fifth grade with two decimal integer is named atomic word group, in each category, there are not many words, a lot of which have only one word that cannot be subdivided any more. With the increasing of the level, the semantic description is more and more detailed.

### 2.2.2 Cilin Coding Improvement

The paper adopts six-level coding system to facilitate the calculation. Two digits encoding is used for each level, and the English letters are encoded in sequence, such as "A" or "a" substituted by "01", "B" or "b" by "02", and postponed in order. The last two bits we call "mark-bit", which is the sixth level in coding system: "=" is substituted by "01", "#" by "02" and "@" by "03". The new coding system is shown in Table 1. For example, "Da15B02#" becomes "040115020202" in new coding system.

**Table 1.** New coding system of Cilin

| Level | 1 | 2 | 3 | 4 | 5 | 6 |
|---|---|---|---|---|---|---|
| Symbol example | D | a | 15 | B | 02 | # |
| Symbol property | Major category | Medium category | Minor category | Word group | Atomic word group | Mark-bit |
| Coding | 04 | 01 | 15 | 02 | 02 | 02 |

### 2.3 BLEUS Based on Cilin

As Cilin focusing on adequacy, the paper proposed a new smoothed BLEU metric, BLEUS-syn, based on Cilin. This metric mainly introduces the synonym match into BLEUS. It smoothed the precision with n = 1 as Formula (3) to maintain the consistency of the n-gram precisions with different n. Also this smoothing technique can avoid the zero matching in candidate translations because of the short translation and abbreviated form. The pseudo code of the BLEUS-syn algorithm is shown as Fig. 2, which contains two main functions: *isSynonym* and *bleuscalculate*.

When two words *content1* and *content2* arrive, the *isSynonym* function will be triggered: (1) It returns index = 1 if *content1* and *content2* are not in Cilin but have the same form; (2) It extracts the twelve-bit-code sets *code1* and *code2* of *content1* and *content2* from "Cilin.xls". It returns index = 1 if the two code sets have the same code.

When the *bleuscalculate* function is triggered, it will smooth unigram firstly in *Ngramprecision* function: (1) Put the candidate after word segmentation *candi* into seg2, and after de-duplication it is put into array *arr[]*; (2) When calculating the minimum number of unigram in candidate *count*, it will replace the unigram *content2* in *seg2* with the *content* in *arr[]* if the two variables get 1 on *isSynonym* function; And

```
1.      // BLEUS based on Cilin (BLEUS -syn)
2.      String: content1; //word in reference
3.      String: content2; //word in candidate
4.
5.      Function Integer isSynonym(content1, content2)
6.      Integer index=0;
7.      if(content1.equals(content2)) index=1;
8.      List<String>list1 = getCodesByContent(content1);
9.      List<String>list2 = getCodesByContent(content2);
10.     for (String code1 : list1)
11.        for (String code2 : list2)
12.           If(code1==code2) index=1;break;
13.        return index;
14.
15.     Function List<String> getCodesByContent(String content)
16.     Map<String, String>result=XLSLoad.getDataFromFile("/Cilin.xls");
17.        for (String key : result.keySet())
18.           String val = result.get(key);
19.     String[] valItem = val.split(" ");
20.     for (String : valItem)
21.        if (string.equals(content)) codes.add(key);break;
22.        return codes;
23.
24.     Function Double: Ngramprecision(ref, candi, N); // N-gram precision of "count 1" smoothing
25.     Function Float: bleuscalculate(ref, candi)
26.     Integer: lr←ref.length(); // length of reference
27.     Integer: lc←candi.length(); // length of candidate
28.
29.     Double:BLEUS4←min(0, (1-lr/lc)) +1/4* (log(Ngramprecision(ref,candi,1)) +
        log(Ngramprecision(ref,candi,2)) + log(Ngramprecision(ref,candi,3))
        + log(Ngramprecision(ref,candi,4)))
30.     Return exp(BLEUS4);
```

**Fig. 2.** BLEUS-syn algorithm.

record the *count* at the same time; (3) The same way, when counting *max_ref_count* it will replace the unigram *content1* in *seg1* with the *content* in *arr[]* if the two variables get 1 on *isSynonym* function; Then put the *seg1* and *seg2* after replacement into *seg11* and *seg22*; (4) Then we get the minimum of *count* and *max_ref_count*, which is called *count_clip*, and calculate the sum of *count_clip* and unigram precision. For N = 2, 3, 4, we obtain the corresponding smoothed precision with *seg11* and *seg22*, and then the final BLEUS value.

BLEUS-syn algorithm has smoothed the traditional BLEU to make the evaluation at sentence level possible. It also has smoothed unigram precision to deal with the zero matching of unigram as a result of short translations and English abbreviations. And the synonym match based on Cilin decreases the precision reduction caused by the diversity of language expression.

## 3  Metric Performance Analysis

### 3.1  Corpus and Environment

In the experiment, we use a publicly available benchmark dataset [9], which contains total 8,848 sentence pairs with Russian-Chinese bilingual alignment from 5 websites in news domain. These sentences are different from each other in the form. They are ranked according to Russian sentence length. We proceed the Russian Chinese online translation on Google[1], Baidu[2], Bing[3] and Youdao[4]and get 4 candidate translations from the 4 online translation systems. The Chinese sentences in corpus are considered as reference translations.

We run the experiment on the computer with 8.00 GB memory and Intel(R) Core (TM) i7-6700HQ CPU. Firstly, we implement the traditional BLEUS algorithm to take the BLEUS of the 4 online translation systems. Secondly, we adopt the synonym match to smooth unigram precision; And then we take the other n-gram matches with the segmentation translations after synonym substitution. Finally, we get the BLEU-syn value.

### 3.2  Result and Discussion

Firstly, we implement the traditional BLEUS algorithm with the test dataset to take the BLEUS through comparing the similarity of reference and 4 candidates. The 4 systems' average BLEUS (BLEUS-word) on the whole test set is shown as Fig. 3.

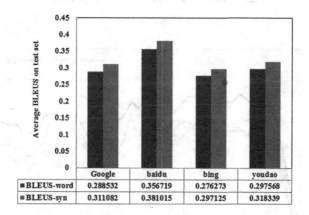

|  | Google | baidu | bing | youdao |
|---|---|---|---|---|
| ■BLEUS-word | 0.288532 | 0.356719 | 0.276273 | 0.297568 |
| ■BLEUS-syn | 0.311082 | 0.381015 | 0.297125 | 0.318339 |

**Fig. 3.** BLEUS evaluation results of 4 systems.

---

[1] http://translate.google.cn/.

[2] http://fanyi.baidu.com/.

[3] https://www.bing.com/translator/.

[4] http://fanyi.youdao.com/.

We take the average of the 200 experimental results as the final result of the group in order to display the results with the chart show. Then we obtain the 45 groups of BLEUS change curve shown as Fig. 4.

Secondly, we implement the BLEUS-syn in the same way with the same corpus to evaluate the translation quality of the 4 systems. We adopt the same experimental process as the BLEUS. Then, we get the results of average BLEUS-syn as shown in Fig. 3 and obtain the 45 groups of BLEUS-syn change curve shown as Fig. 5.

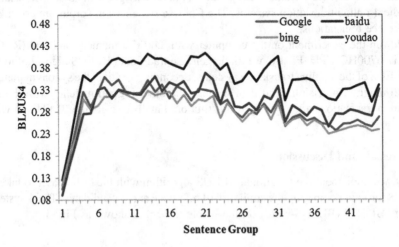

**Fig. 4.** BLEUS change curves of 4 systems.

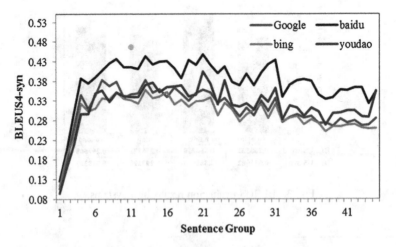

**Fig. 5.** BLEUS-syn change curves of 4 systems.

Finally, we compare the experimental results of the BLEUS-syn and the traditional BLEUS. Figures 4 and 5 present the average BLEUS and BLEUS-syn results. The horizontal coordinate is the sentence group sequence and the vertical coordinates are the traditional BLEUS4 and BLEUS4-syn scores respectively. The two figures show that the evaluation results of BLEUS and BLEUS-syn are consistent: (1) The two algorithms' average BLEUS4 have the same trend in the whole range; (2) Baidu system performance is the best and its BLEUS4 score is the highest; Youdao performance is slightly worse than Baidu, but better than that of Google; the translation quality of Bing is the worst and its BLEUS4 score is the lowest; (3) The score of BLEUS4 was lower in the first few groups, and then this value increases dramatically with the increase of sentence length. The main reason is that there may be English abbreviations or short translation when the sentence length is short, so that the candidate match with the reference worse, the n-gram matched will be less and the BLEUS4 is reduced. But the value of BLEUS4 tends to be stable with the increase of the sentence length.

Figure 3 shows that, in the whole test set, (1) The evaluation value of BLEUS-syn is higher than that of the traditional BLEUS for the 4 online systems; (2) The 4 systems on Russian Chinese translation is consistent that Baidu performance is the best, Youdao the second, Google the third and Bing is the worst; (3) When using the synonym match based on Cilin, the BLEUS value of Baidu increases from 0.356719 to 0.381015, with an increase of 6.81%; the BLEUS value of Youdao increases from 0.297568 to 0.318339, with an increase of 6.98%; the Google BLEUS is increased by 7.82% from 0.288532 to 0.311082; the one of Bing is increased by 7.55% from 0.276273 to 0.297125; (4) we use longitudinal comparison to compare the performance of different smoothing algorithms based on the same evaluation metric-BLEU; and we only apply the average BLEU value for evaluation, which is convenient and clear, and conducive to the evaluation metric performance parameters' adjustment and optimization; This will greatly save resources and time, and improve the efficiency; We will apply horizontal comparison for different types of metrics; (5) Google performance improves the most and Baidu the least; this result will play a very good role in the system integration.

We adopt longitudinal comparison to evaluate the performance of BLEUS and BLEUS-syn in the above experiment. The quality of these evaluation metrics is usually measured by determining the correlation of the scores assigned by the evaluation metrics to scores assigned by a human evaluation metric, most commonly fluency and adequacy. In this paper, Pearson correlation coefficient $r_{xy}$ is used to evaluate the two measurements. The higher the coefficient, the better the performance of the evaluation metric.

Suppose the data point on test set, which includes variable automatic scoring x and manual scoring y, is set to $\{(x_i, y_i)\}$. Then the Pearson correlation coefficient $r_{xy}$ is defined as follows:

$$r_{xy} = \frac{\sum_i (x_i - \bar{x})(y_i - \bar{y})}{\sqrt{\sum_i (x_i - \bar{x})^2 \sum_i (y_i - \bar{y})^2}} \tag{5}$$

$\bar{x} = \frac{1}{n}\sum_{i=1}^{n} x_i$ and $\bar{y} = \frac{1}{n}\sum_{i=1}^{n} y_i$ are the averages of sample X and Y respectively. The variable $n$ is the source sentences number of test set. The correlation coefficient $r_{xy}$ does not depend on sample size [10]. Its value ranges from $-1$ to 1. The positive correlation

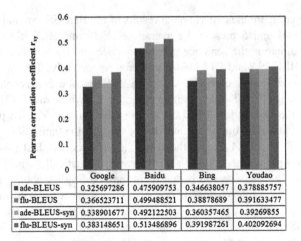

| | Google | Baidu | Bing | Youdao |
|---|---|---|---|---|
| ■ ade-BLEUS | 0.325697286 | 0.475909753 | 0.346638057 | 0.378885757 |
| ■ flu-BLEUS | 0.366523711 | 0.499488521 | 0.38878689 | 0.391633477 |
| ■ ade-BLEUS-syn | 0.338901677 | 0.492122503 | 0.360357465 | 0.39269855 |
| ■ flu-BLEUS-syn | 0.383148651 | 0.513486896 | 0.391987261 | 0.402092694 |

**Fig. 6.** Pearson correlation coefficient $r_{xy}$ between the automatic score and human scores of adequacy and fluency.

coefficient indicates that variable X and variable Y tend to increase or decrease at the same time. On the contrary, the negative correlation coefficient indicates that the variable Y will decrease with the increase of the variable X or increase with the decrease of X.

Take the 4 Russian-Chinese machine translation systems with BLEUS and BLEUS-syn to get the Pearson correlation coefficient $r_{xy}$ between the automatic evaluation score and human scores of adequacy and fluency, which is shown in Fig. 6.

As can be seen in Fig. 6, the Pearson correlation coefficient of adequacy and fluency are all improved as using the Cilin-based SST algorithm for the traditional BLEUS method. For example, the adequacy correlation coefficient of Baidu increases from 0.475910 to 0.492123, Google from 0.325697 to 0.338902, Youdao from 0.378886 to 0.392699, and that of Bing from 0.346638 to 0.360357. And the fluency correlation coefficient is the same. Use of synonym matching does not influence the fluency of candidate translation and simultaneously improve the adequacy of the translation. And the translation is still readable.

The results of the longitudinal comparisons above are consistent with the results of the human evaluation. The above experiment results show that the longitudinal comparison method to evaluate the metrics with different parameter settings based on the same method is effective. This method is conducive to the adjustment and optimization of evaluation metrics, and is more convenient. Also it can significantly save energy and time and improve the timeliness.

In this paper, we use the significance test to verify the effectivity of experimental results. Also, this method can be applied to the offline open source system. It can greatly enhance the MT system performance in the case of the corpus size is not limited. The BLEUS-syn algorithm can greatly improve the performance of traditional BLEUS algorithm. And it plays a very good role in the MT evaluation with Chinese as the target language.

In this paper, we use the significance test to verify the effectivity of experimental results. Also, this method can be applied to the offline open source system. It can greatly enhance the MT system performance in the case of the corpus size is not limited. The BLEUS-syn algorithm can greatly improve the performance of traditional BLEUS algorithm. And it plays a very good role in the MT evaluation with Chinese as the target language.

# 4    Conclusion

This paper proposes an improved smoothed BLEU evaluation metric (BLEUS-syn). This metric has smoothed n-gram of the traditional BLEUS in the light of zero matching caused by English abbreviations or short translation, and introduced synonym match in unigram matching, and then calculated the other n-gram precisions. The results of the new algorithm and the traditional BLEUS algorithm are consistent from the longitudinal comparison. It will greatly enhance the performance of traditional BLEUS algorithm, especially in machine translation with Chinese as target language.

Further research will concern that the relevant word in Cilin, HowNet and other metrics with synonym match such as ROUGE, METEOR. Also we will evaluate these different types of metrics with horizontal comparison, for example, ORANGE and traditional human evaluation.

**Acknowledgments.** The research is supported by the Key Project of State Language Commission of China (Resource Construction and Application of Low-Resource Languages for the 21st Century Maritime Silk Road) and the Featured Innovation Project of Guangdong Province (No. 2015KTSCX035).

# References

1. Assessment Specifications of Machine Translation Systems. GF 2006
2. Yu, S.: Automatic evaluation of output quality for Machine Translation systems. Mach. Transl. **8**, 117–126 (1993)
3. Papineni, K., Roukos, S., Ward, T., et al.: BLEU: a method for automatic evaluation of machine translation. In: Proceedings of the 40th Annual Meeting of the Association for Computational Linguistics 2002, pp. 311–318 (2002)
4. Lin, C.Y., Och, F.J.: ORANGE: a method for evaluating automatic evaluation metrics for machine translation. In: Proceedings of COLING-2004 (2004)
5. Lin, C.Y.: ROUGE: a package for automatic evaluation of summaries. In: Proceedings of Workshop on Text Summarization Branches Out, Post-conference Workshop of ACL 2004 (2004)
6. Banerjee, S., Lavie, A.: Meteor: an automatic metric for MT evaluation with improved correlation with human judgments. In: ACL Workshop on Intrinsic and Extrinsic Evaluation Measures for MT and/or Summarization (2005)
7. Mei, J., Zhu, Y., Gao, Y., et al.: Tongyici Cilin (Extended). HIT IR-Lab (1996)

8. Chen, B., Cherry, C.: A systematic comparison of smoothing techniques for sentence-level BLEU. In: Proceedings of the Ninth Workshop on Statistical Machine Translation 2014, pp. 362–367 (2014)
9. Du, W., Liu, W., Yu, J., et al.: Russian-Chinese sentence-level aligned news corpus. In: EAMT 2015 (2015)
10. Koehn, P.: Moses-statistical machine translation system- user manual and code guide (2015)

# Research on the Calculation Method of Semantic Similarity Based on Concept Hierarchy

Kai Wang[⊠]

Department of Health Management, Bengbu Medical College,
Bengbu 233000, China
wangkai0552@126.com

**Abstract.** In this paper, for the low similarity computation accuracy of concept in the field of domain ontology mapping, formal concept analysis theory and rough set theory are introduced to similarity computation. Jointly considering attribute hierarchies in concept lattice, the semantic hierarchy of the concepts are weighted differently, and the theory and methods of semantic similarity based on concept hierarchy is given. Finally, similarity computing model is prospected. Experimental results show the model has a high computational accuracy.

**Keywords:** Semantic similarity · Attribute hierarchies · Concept lattice

## 1 Introduction

With the explosive growth of knowledge, representation, sharing and exchanging of which has become urgent to solve. Ontology is a shared concept of a clear explanation standardization, which makes it possible to resolve all these issues. It has increasingly become important component of knowledge engineering. Formal concept analysis theory is a mathematical method put by Professor Willie R, which comes from the understanding of concept related to the areas of philosophy, and reflects the hierarchy between the concepts.

Rough set theory is a theory of data analysis proposed by Z. Pawlak, which uses the approximate relationship between the upper and lower use of data to describe the uncertainty of information. Now has been widely used in decision analysis, pattern recognition, machine learning and knowledge discovery.

Wu Qiang broadens the scope of formal concept in the paper [1], applying rough set to Formal concept analysis area, to definite the concept which cannot be studied. Yang wen-ping discusses the rough approximation of formal concept, proposing to use the rough set method to solve the upper and lower approximation of rough concept, which theoretically proves that the result of this theory is equivalent to the approximate extension of other ones. Kent gives the analysis of the approximate operator model of

Fund projects: Key Project of AnHui Education Department (KJ2015B023by); Key Project of Bengbu Medical College (BYKY1409ZD).

concept lattice, illustrates the relationship between the approximation operators. Shao [2] synthesizes the basic rough model and reduction concept lattice model, getting the corresponding functional dependency algorithms, by the theory of rough set operations [3]. The phenomenon of missing values is a widespread problem in knowledge engineering, which mainly related to the expression and processing of uncertain concepts [4]. With the rapid development of the Semantic Web, the number of domain ontology gradually increases, to some extent, which seriously affects the sharing and reuse of knowledge between domain ontologies.

Ontology mapping is an effective method to solve the problem foregoing, the key of which is to get conceptual similarity [5]. Due to the reasons above-mentioned, this article uses upper and lower approximation of rough set theory, proposes rough formal concept in missing-value context, put forward the improved theory and methods for similarity calculation of rough formal concept in missing-value context.

## 2 Related Concepts

### 2.1 Rough Set Theory

Rough Set Theory is some kind of mathematical tool dealing with fuzzy and uncertain knowledge. The main idea of this theory is to access decision-making or classification rules, in the premise of maintaining the same classification, by knowledge reduction [6]. Rough Set Theory generally refers to some undefined subset, regularly be approximation defined by two precision sets (upper approximation and lower approximation).

**Definition 1.** For a given knowledge base $K = (U, R)$, U refers to non-empty set of objects; R is a family of equivalence relations based on U. If $P \subseteq R$, and P are not empty, then the intersection of all equivalence relations in P set is also an equivalence relation, called indiscernibility relations. For each subset $X \subseteq U$ and equivalence relation R, we can get these as follows:

$$\underline{R}X = \cup \{Y \in U/R | Y \subseteq X\} \tag{1}$$

$$\overline{R}X = \cup \{Y \in U/R | Y \cap X \neq \emptyset\}. \tag{2}$$

They are called the upper approximation and lower approximation of relation P respectively. If the upper and lower approximation are not equal, X is called the rough set of R, otherwise, called the defined or precise set of R [7].

### 2.2 Theory of Formal Concept Analysis

Formal Concept Analysis are widely used in many area, such as data analysis and rule extraction, the core of which is the concept lattice, that is the concept hierarchy based on binary relation. Concepts exist in the form of relations of posts in the lattice. For each concept, they are composed of extensions and intensions of their own. The relationship of the concept of upper and lower nodes is the one of father and son. The concept hierarchy between concepts can be clearly seen by the Hasse map. The visualization of data could be easily got.

**Definition 2.** There is a set of L, and a, b, c ∈ L, the prerequisites that binary relation ≤ is the poset of L are: (1) a ≤ a (reflexivity); (2) a ≤ b and b ≤ a ⇒ a = b (anti-symmetry); (3) a ≤ b and b ≤ c ⇒ a ≤ c (transitivity).

**Definition 3** (Infimum and Supremum). There is a subset S ∈ L in the poset (L, ≤), and then arbitrary element in set L is called the lower bound of subset S. And if it contains a largest element, we call it Infimum; similarly, the definition of Supremum could be got.

**Definition 4** (Lattice). The poset (L, ≤) can be called Lattice only if it could Satisfy the following requirements: (1) For any a, b ∈ L, a ∧ b and a ∨ b are both exist; (2) Infimum and Supremum are presence for any a, b ∈ L.

## 2.3 Missing-Value Context and Rough Formal Concept

Ordinary formal context K = (G, M, I) is a triple context, G is a set of objects, M is a set of attributes, and I is a binary relation such that $I \subseteq G \times M$, and it is identified. However, in real life due to lack of information or unpredictable cases happening, knowledge we need cannot be obtained in the normal way, which makes it hard to express. Based on the reasons above it is necessary to take specially steps to deal with these problems [8]. First of all, the definition of missing-value context is given. When the relationship between certain object g and property m is uncertain, I ⊆ (g, m) not being judged, it could be called being missing-value [9].

**Definition 5** (Missing-Value Context). Missing-Value Context T = (U, A, R) is a triple context, U = {o1, o2 … on} is a set of objects, A = {a1, a2 … an} is set of Attributes. R is an uncertain relationship between U and A [10].

Better to explain the definition of rough formal concept, formal concept is given firstly.

**Definition 6** (Formal Concept). For a given formal context K = (G, M, I), concept (A, B) is called Formal Concept, if it satisfies the conditions that (1) A ∈ G, B ∈ M; (2) (A, B) ∈ I; (3) A′ = B, B′ = A, among which A′ represents the shared attribute sets of objects A, B′ is on behalf of the shared object sets of attributes B.

**Definition 7** (Rough Formal Concept). For a given Missing-Value Context T = (U, A, R), only if the concept meets the conditions as follows, it could be named Rough Formal Concept: (1) A ∈ G, B ∈ M; (2) A × B is a rough set based on relation I.

# 3   Traditional Similarity Calculation Model

Comprehensive analysis of domestic and foreign literature, the existing techniques and methods focus on solving the problem of semantic visual concept set, combined with a variety of algorithms. The concept of re clustering, which contains a number of additional concepts. So as to achieve the concept of semantic image annotation, unsupervised image distance measurement problem is to eliminate regional similarity. The concept contained in the visual concept set is an important factor to determine the classification accuracy of the image scene, the capacity of the assembly to reduce the scene classification speed. When the capacity is too small, it may cause the decline of classification accuracy. The main problem is that there is no mapping between the underlying feature and the upper level of the image, which leads to the error between the information of the feature expression and the actual semantic.

Therefore, it is necessary to establish the mapping relationship between the underlying visual concepts and the upper level semantic relations. On the other hand, the concept of the right amount can not only guarantee the time efficiency of classified search, but also is easy to implement the mulch-level classification model. Therefore it is necessary to set up the concept of semantic level set, dynamically adjust the classification granularity, get the concept of vector reduction set, and realize the classification performance of image semantics.

## 3.1   Tversky Ratio Model

Tversky measured the degree of similarity between concepts by using the shared feature sets of entities. The computational model is as follows [11]:

$$Sin(m,n) = \frac{f(M \cap N)}{f(M \cap N) + \alpha \cdot f(M - N) + \beta \cdot f(N - M)} \quad (3)$$

Among which Sin (m, n) denotes the similarity between concept m and n; M and N are the feature sets of m and n; f is the metric function of feature sets; (M − N) indicates the feature sets which lies in M rather than in N; Similarly, (N − M) indicates the feature sets which lies in N rather than in M; Parameter $\alpha$, $\beta$ adjust the cases dealing with the asymmetric feature sets.

## 3.2   The Similarity Calculation Model Based on Formal Concept Analysis

Based on the Tversky Ratio Model, the similarity calculation model to the basis of Formal Concept Analysis is proposed by Souza and Davis, which uses the mathematical operation $\wedge$ and $\vee$ to calculate the irreducible infimum [12].

$$Sin(m,n) = \frac{|(m \vee n)^{\wedge}|}{|(m \vee n)^{\wedge}| + \alpha |(m - n)^{\wedge}| + (1 - \alpha)|(n - m)^{\wedge}|} \quad (4)$$

m ∧ n represents the supremum of formal concept m and n; $(m \wedge n)^{\wedge}$ means the element sets of irreducible infimum of the supremum features; $(m - n)^{\wedge}$ denotes the irreducible infimum element sets which lies in m instead of n; and vice versa.

### 3.3   The Similarity Calculation Model Based on Information

Based on the Tversky Ratio Model, Formica put forward the similarity calculation model that based on information, which makes use of the similar map of concepts in domain knowledge.

$$\text{Sin}((M1, N1), (M2, N2)) = \frac{|M1 \cap M2|}{\lambda} \times \omega + [\frac{1}{\theta} \bullet \max(\sum_{<m,n> \in P} f(m,n))] \times (1 - \omega) \quad (5)$$

M1 ∩ N1 is the number of the same objects in the pairs of the concepts; $\lambda$ is the bigger value to be compared with the numerical objects; $\theta$ is the larger value to be compared with the numerical attributes; $\sum_{<m,n> \in P} f(m,n)$ is the summation of the concepts whose attributes matches one another in the concept similarity map; $\omega$ is the weighting factor adjusting different cases.

It is not difficult to draw conclusions from the model above that many scholars just improved the model raised by Tversky. The semantic meaning of similarity model is enriched by pulling in the Rough Set Theory and Formal Concept Analysis. But there are still limitations, specifically expressed in two aspects: (1) simply counting the numbers of upper concept nodes, lacking of accuracy measurement, (2) no consideration about the differences between the feature properties of different concept level, only depending on computing the semantic distance between concepts to determine the value of similarity.

### 3.4   Feature Matrix Filtering

The characteristic matrix filtering classification module using the experimental image local feature information, calculate the frequency of visual concepts, the concept of annotation selected frequency is higher than the average word frequency of image concept, denoted as the number 1 [13]. the semantic information of such images can be approximated by the concept of visual, ergodic concept set, the remaining part is a value of 0, finally through the numerical normalization method, the characteristic matrix of various classification database into a feature vector corresponding to visual concepts, test image feature vector and classification of library image features to calculate the Euclidean distance weight, the minimum distance of neighbor statistics marked concept of minimum, and the final output image of the scene the closest image classification category base number [14].

Feature matrix filtering classification algorithm, the specific process description, such as Algorithm 1.

**Algorithm 1. feature matrix filter classification algorithm**

```
Input: array set, experimental image set,
Output: Image Classification Library serial number
1 calculate the frequency of the occurrence of the
visual concept word, the frequency of the statistical
concept word, form the concept word frequency array;
2 traversal frequency array, the frequency of each ar-
ray to calculate the mean;
3 the comparison of the numerical value is larger than
the concept of the mean of the word, and marked 1, the
remaining concept of the word mark is 0;
4 the Euclidean distance between the feature vector of
the test image and the feature vector group of the
Classification Library is calculated;
5 statistical distance of the smallest tagging concept,
the output image classification library serial number.
```

# 4  Rough Formal Concept Similarity Calculation Model

## 4.1  Irreducible Supremum and Infimum in Formal Concept Analysis

The theory of concept lattice as a formal tool of knowledge representation can directly show the structural characteristics of the domain knowledge and the classification, inside the objects and attributes of concept nodes, which can be represented by a set of objects node extension, attribute set by the nodes within the culvert structure. The hierarchical structure of concept lattice is easy to represent the domain concept relation with different granularity [15].

Formal concept is formed of objects and attributes, which can determine the equivalence relation of the object G and attribute M by the formal context K = (G, M, I). For every non-empty set of formal concept, there always exists the sole largest sub-concept and smallest parent concept, which is called supremum and infimum. If it existing the only element not expressed by the largest sub-concept of others, it is named Irreducible supremum element; similarly, it is easy to get the definition of irreducible infimum element.

## 4.2  Conceptual Semantic Classification Model

The concept of semantic classification problem can be transformed into solving the minimization problem, whose core is to use the feature information acquisition and semantic quantification in the training sample set in the decomposition of local features, combined with the concept of clustering initialization word set. Through semantic measurement of the distance between the sample words set. In this paper, we use the hierarchical classification model of concept lattice to map the object set and attribute set of the concept lattice nodes, and the semantic feature vector corresponding to the two elements of the formal context.

The relation of feature information can be expressed by the collar matrix Mat, if the set of the non-edge graph is the set of nodes, which represents the concept set. The definition of any two node, if the node to meet the boundary between the inter node, node friends. The undirected graph represented by the collar matrix satisfies the symmetry and the commutative property.

This paper proposes the conversion algorithm of random stratified form background based on adjacency matrix, the algorithm initializes the formal context, concept node is added to the random object set and attribute set, judgment on whether any node to meet friends node relationship, if meet this relationship, the relationship between the nodes corresponding to the I is set to 1, and the 0. Traverse to all nodes, repeat the process, can get the formal background (O, A, I), the specific process description, such as Algorithm 2.

### Algorithm 2. Based on the collar matrix of random hierarchical background conversion algorithm

**Input**: Non edge graph set $G = (V, E)$, Collar matrix $Mat = (m_{ij})$

**Output**: Formal context (O, A, I)

```
1   Begin        O = ∅,  A = ∅
2       For   each  v ∈ V
3           Add  v  to  {o₁,o₂,.....};  Add  v  to  4 {u₁,u₂,.....}
5   Endfor
6       For   each  v
7           IF    mᵢⱼ = 1
8               Then    (oᵢ,uⱼ) ∈ I
9           EndIf
10  Endfor
11  End
```

### 4.3   Improved Rough Concept Lattice Similarity Calculation Model

On the one hand, by observing the structure of the Hasse map, we know that the included attributes of the upper parent node in concept lattice is the minimal subset attributes of the lower sub-class nodes. And if two nodes have the same feature properties, the conclusion that they must have the same upper parent node can be got. On the other hand, from the taxonomic point of view, the similarity degree between underlying object is higher than the one between upper layer object.

Concept lattice module collects the related medical concepts, which describes the concept of classification as the same class and sets up the scene library; local features are based on the concept of concept words obtaining different categories by hierarchical clustering method set. According to the statistical distribution of the set of concepts, feature matrix obtain the characteristic information of concepts, clustering to get the concept set; Using concept lattice incremental algorithms, it is respectively using from the scene of concept lattice, the lattice structure, and the dynamic adjustment of the concept of extension parameters to obtain with an array of annotation word set reduction.

Concept lattice construction algorithm is the specific process description, which can be descried as Algorithm 3.

### Algorithm 3. Concept lattice construction algorithm based on formal context of visual word set

```
Input: classification map training set, image receive
matrix, classification dimension
Output: array set
Begin
1 get the local characteristics of the set of the
classification map
2 each For,
3 adjust the classification set, to generate mufti-
dimensional image matrix
4 set attribute to Maps grid and node attribute set
5 While
6 End for
 7 eliminate redundant information of all kinds of XOR
training sets feature vector
8 IF any set of feature vectors,
9  delete Then
10 meet the requirements of dynamic adjustment of con-
cept of extension parameters, so that the form of ob-
ject of the same dimension could be defined as the
background,
11 get types of training sets of generating in concept
lattice structure
12  obtain the reduction array on the basis of grid
attribute hierarchy
13 EndIf
14 Endfor
15 End
```

Based on the above analysis, semantic parameters of the upper layer is greater than the one of the lower layer. The improved rough concept lattice similarity calculation model is given below.

$$f_{RSIM} = ((A_{1\_}, B_{1\_}), (A_{2\_}, B_{2\_})) = \frac{|A_{1\_} \cap A_{2\_}|}{\gamma} \times \alpha + \frac{\sum_{i=1}^{n} X_i W_i}{\sum_{i=1}^{n} Y_i W_i} \times (1 - \alpha) \quad (6)$$

Specific parameters are defined as follows: $X_i = fi(B_{1\_} \cap B_{2\_})$ represents the shared property features of the rough concept lattice in level i; $Y_i = fi(B_{1\_} \cap B_{2\_}) + fi(B_{1\_} - B_{2\_}) + fi(B_{2\_} - B_{1\_})$ denotes the property features of the rough concept lattice in level i; $W_i$ means the weight of the conceptual elements in level i. $A_{1\_}$ is the lower approximation concept $(A_{1\_}, B_{1\_})$'s object, while $(A_{1\_}, B_{1\_})$ is the rough formal concept of $(A1, B1)$, so as $A_{2\_}$; $B_{1\_}$ is the upper approximation concept $(A_{1\_}, B_{1\_})$'s attribute; Parameter $\alpha$ is the weighting factor adjusting accuracy of the model. The weight of the different level is determined by $1/2i - 1$, known through the literature [4], among which i stands for the number of the level. In order to better explain the model above, a formal context of domain ontology modeling is given below, shown as Table 1.

**Table 1.** Formal context of the domain ontology

|    | A(D) | A(L) | A(B) | A(J) | A(F) |
|----|------|------|------|------|------|
| P1 | ×    |      | ×    |      |      |
| P2 | ×    |      | ×    |      |      |
| P3 |      | ×    | ×    |      | ×    |
| P4 |      | ×    | ×    |      |      |
| P5 |      |      |      | ×    |      |

|    | A(E) | A(K) | A(R) | A(M) | A(H) |
|----|------|------|------|------|------|
| P1 | ×    |      |      |      | ×    |
| P2 | ×    |      |      |      | ×    |
| P3 |      | ×    |      |      |      |
| P4 |      |      | ×    |      | ×    |
| P5 |      |      |      | ×    | ×    |

Based on the literature [4], the generating algorithm for building concept lattice to the basis of matrix column rank with attribute priority, by which uses the matrix column rank of the concept and the union operation of the concept pairs to generate rough formal concepts having hierarchical structure. The hierarchical concepts corresponding with Table 1 are just as follows.

Layer 1: C1$(G, \emptyset)$;
Layer 2: C2{{P1, P2, P4, P5}, {A(H) }}, C3{{P1, P2, P3, P4}, {A(B)}};
Layer 3: C4{{P1, P2, P4}, {A(H), A(B) }}, C5{{P1, P2, P5}, {A(E) }};
Layer 4: C6{{P1, P2}, {A(H), A(B), A(E), A(D)}}, C7{{P3, P4}, {A(L), A(B)}};
Layer 5: C8{{P5}, {A(D), A(H), A(E), A(J) }}, C9{{P3}, {A(L), A(F), A(K), A(B) }}, C10{{P4}, {A(L), A(H), A(M), A(R), A(B)}};
Layer 6: C11$(\emptyset, M)$

**Table 2.** Property values of the related levels

| Layer 1 | A(H), A(B) | Weight: 1 |
|---------|------------|-----------|
| Layer 2 | A(E) | Weight: 1/2 |
| Layer 3 | A(L), A(D) | Weight: 1/4 |
| Layer 4 | A(L), A(F), A(K), A(B) | Weight: 1/8 |

The rough formal concept with the hierarchical structure is generated just as the map 1. The weight of different layers is given in Table 2. Using the formula above, the similarity between the concept nodes can be calculated. For example, the similarity value between concept C2 and C6 is got by setting the parameter $\alpha = 0.25$.

$$f_{RSIM(C_2,C_6)} = \frac{2}{4} \times 0.25 + \frac{1 \times 1 + 0 \times \frac{1}{2} + 0 \times \frac{1}{4} + 0 \times \frac{1}{8}}{(1+3) \times 1 + (0+1) \times \frac{1}{2} + (0+1) \times \frac{1}{4} + (0+0) \times \frac{1}{8}} = 0.34 \quad (7)$$

By using this similarity measure, all the objects and attributes which are non-empty could be calculated. In order to analyze these data we get, the result of the improved model and the one of the Souza model are put together to make comparison shown as the Table 3. The table is divided into two parts by the diagonal of the number one. The value of the upper triangular is the result of the improved similarity of rough formal concepts. The value of the lower triangular is the result of the similarity of the Souza model.

**Table 3.** Values of the similarity between concepts

|  | $C_2$ | $C_3$ | $C_4$ | $C_5$ | $C_6$ | $C_7$ | $C_8$ | $C_9$ | $C_{10}$ |
|----------|----|----|----|----|----|----|----|----|----|
| $C_2$ | 1 | 0.1 | 0.6 | 0.1 | 0.3 | 0.1 | 0.6 | 0.0 | 0.4 |
| $C_3$ | 0.0 | 1 | 0.6 | 0.1 | 0.4 | 0.9 | 0.0 | 0.4 | 0.4 |
| $C_4$ | 0.6 | 0.6 | 1 | 0.1 | 0.9 | 0.5 | 0.3 | 0.4 | 0.9 |
| $C_5$ | 0.0 | 0.0 | 0.0 | 1 | 0.4 | 0.0 | 0.5 | 0.0 | 0.0 |
| $C_6$ | 0.4 | 0.4 | 0.7 | 0.4 | 1 | 0.3 | 0.6 | 0.4 | 0.8 |
| $C_7$ | 0.0 | 0.7 | 0.5 | 0.0 | 0.3 | 1 | 0.0 | 0.9 | 0.8 |
| $C_8$ | 0.4 | 0.0 | 0.3 | 0.4 | 0.5 | 0.0 | 1 | 0.0 | 0.3 |
| $C_9$ | 0.0 | 0.4 | 0.3 | 0.0 | 0.3 | 0.7 | 0.0 | 1 | 0.4 |
| $C_{10}$ | 0.4 | 0.4 | 0.7 | 0.0 | 0.5 | 0.7 | 0.3 | 0.5 | 1 |

## 5  Model Analysis

For the reason that precision and recall always changes with the mutative thresholds, they cannot be used to analyze the result of the similarity accurately. Based on the values in Table 3, the concept node in the high-level such as C2 and its child node C4 are chosen to analyze the relationship between other concept nodes. Compared to the Souza model, the conclusion that the improved model is better could be got at two aspects. On the one hand, the result of accuracy is improved. The values of the improved model increase to the different degrees, for jointly considering attribute hierarchies in concept lattice and the relations between objects and attributes. On the other hand, irrelevant concept pairs decrease. Due to the concepts in the domain area have certain similar characteristics, all the values of the concept pairs could not be zero. The improved model cuts down the number of the pairs with zero effectively, enhancing the measurement accuracy between concept pairs.

Experimental selection of different concept word capacity and concept extension threshold will directly affect the accuracy of image classification. The concept of word capacity set is large, the concept of the word set in useless word easy to appear, the visual description ability is low, the accuracy of classification results is not high, with decreasing capacity limit, the more likely to describe the concept of different expression of the same scene. This model can effectively reduce the synonymous expression of the concept of description, but the accuracy of the algorithm is related to the capacity value. When the value exceeds the ideal range, the classification accuracy is more significant.

The concept of the extension of the threshold will directly affect the concept of the formal context, resulting in the concept of effective visual node is too concentrated or loose. When the extension threshold is smaller, the effective visual concept node focused on concept lattice structure of low layer, describe the concept of synonymous expression is evident, the classification accuracy is low; when the extension threshold is greater, the effective visual concept node focused on concept lattice structure is high, the number of nodes is less effective, easy to cause the characteristic of node loss. Due to the single concept expression ability is low, the scene classification is rough, the classification accuracy is relatively low.

This method dynamically adjusts the capacity limit and the extension of the concept of concepts from different levels of threshold. Concept lattice node, semantic concept matrix of multilevel cross can be also improved, in the precondition of reducing the size of the calculation, which effectively improve the classification accuracy of the image scene.

## 6 Conclusions and Future Work

The paper puts forward the theory and methods for similarity calculation of rough formal concept in missing-value content, in which formal concept analysis theory and rough set theory are introduced to similarity computation. Jointly considering attribute hierarchies in concept lattice, the semantic hierarchies of the concepts are weighted differently. Experimental results show the model has a high computational accuracy. The model above proposes a practical theory and methods to merge domain ontology, helping to raising the accuracy of ontology integration.

## References

1. Wu, Q., Liu, Z.: The rough concept in FCA. J. Chin. Comput. Syst. **26**, 1563–1565 (2014). Beijing
2. Shao, M.: Set approximations in fuzzy formal concept analysis. Fuzzy Sets Syst., 2627–2640 (2013). Beijing

3. Xie, Z., Liu, Z.: Concept analysis knowledge acquisition in missing-context. Comput. Sci., 36–39 (2010). Beijing
4. Mao, H.: An algorithm of concept lattice based on matrix column rank with attribute priority. J. Hebei Univ., 130–133 (2009). Baoding
5. Kesorn, K., Poslad, S.: An enhanced bag of visual words vector space model to represent visual content in athletics images. IEEE Trans. Multimedia **14**(1), 211–222 (2012)
6. Tang, Y., Xu, D., et al.: A novel image scene classification method based on category topic simplex. J. Graph. **15**(7), 1067–1073 (2010)
7. Fernando, B., Fremont, E.: Supervised learning of Gaussian mixture models for visual vocabulary. Pattern Recognit. **45**, 897–907 (2012)
8. Wang, Y., Li, Y., Gao, W.: Detecting visual words. J. Beijing Inst. Technol. **28**(5), 410–413 (2008). Beijing
9. Maree, R., Denis, P., et al.: Incremental Indexing and Distributed Image Search Using Shared Randomized Vocabularies, pp. 91–100. ACM Press, New York (2010)
10. Sanchez, J., Perronnin, F., et al.: Image classification with the fisher vector: theory and practice. Int. J. Comput. Vision **105**(3), 222–245 (2013)
11. Yuan, W., Tao, J., et al.: Information retrieval and data mining based on open network knowledge. J. Comput. Res. Dev. **52**(2), 456–474 (2014)
12. Lazabnik, S., Schmid, C., Ponce, J.: Beyond bag of features: pyramid matching for recognizing natural scene categories. In: IEEE Conference on Computer Vision and Pattern Recognition, New York, pp. 2169–2178 (2006)
13. Li, F., Perona, P.: Abayesian hierarchical model for learning natural scene categories. In: IEEE International Conference on Computer and Pattern Recognition, San Diego, pp. 524–531 (2005)
14. Emrah, E., Nadiz, A.: Scene classification using spatial pyramid of latent topics. In: 20th International Conference on Pattern Recognition, Istanbul, pp. 3603–3606 (2010)
15. Liu, S.Y., Xu, D., Feng, S.H., Liu, D.: A novel visual words definition algorithm of image patch based on semantic information. Acta Electronica Sinica **38**(5), 1156–1161 (2010)

# Author Index

Printed in the United States
By Bookmasters

Printed in the United States
By Bookmasters